> "The miracle of Texas lies in the fact that it is the work of a handful of men. In not a single fight during the entire period from 1800 to 1845 did they muster as many as one thousand fighting men. Overwhelming odds never discouraged them and defeat but spurred them to ultimate victory."
>
> Jack C. Butterfield

TXSG Member Handbook

"Texans Serving Texas"

2017
Edition

Contents

--- Components and Missions 7
--- TXSG Chain-of-Command & Leadership 11
--- Where Does the TXSG Get Its Authority 13
--- Texas, History, and the TXSG 17
--- Modern Era TXSG Deployments 29
--- TXSG Rank Structures 38
--- Dress and Appearance 41
--- Activation Go-Bag 42
--- Force Protection and Anti-Terrorism 46
--- Shelter Operations 49
--- The Media and the Public 52
--- Emergency Management 58
--- Dangerous Texas Wildlife 64
--- Communications 72
--- Phonetic Alphabet 82
--- Guard Duty 89
--- Common Hand And Arm Signals 93
--- Customs and Courtesies 96
--- Hurricanes and Tornados 103
--- TXSG Email Usage 109
--- Fundamentals Of Land Navigation 111

- Operating on the Texas/Mexico Border 122
- Federal Emergency Management Agency 124
- Common Spanish Words and Phrases 128
- Firearms Identification & Safety 130
- Self-Aid and Buddy Care 135
- Compression Only CPR 146
- Height and Weight Table 151
- Tax Implications 153
- Common TXSG Jargon and Abbreciations 155
- TXSG Benefits and Information 157
- About This Handbook 161

Thank You for Volunteering

We obviously do not serve the Texas State Guard for the money because this, generally, costs us more than we make, but we serve for the honor of serving something larger than ourselves. Thank you for serving our Great State of Texas. We come from many backgrounds, many of us come by way of other States; just as did Stephen F. Austin, Davy Crockett, Sam Houston, and many other great Texans. Many of us proudly served in the US Military, but now we are all willing to serve **OUR** State. For that, we earn the title of being called Texas State Guardsmen, and most importantly, "Texans".

This Handbook is written for members of one Texas State Guard (TXSG) unit as a guide for common, helpful, information and tasks. It is not a TXSG-wide "official" handbook required to be followed by TXSG Sr. leadership. Because the Army, Air, and TMAR components operate in differing manners, refer to your unit and utilize their specific methods of completing tasks in the event of conflict with this guide."

Texas State Guard Mission

The mission of the Texas State Guard (TXSG) is to provide mission-ready military forces to assist State and local authorities in times of State emergencies; to conduct homeland security and community service activities under the umbrella of Defense Support to Civil Authorities; and to augment the Texas Army National Guard and Texas Air National Guard as required.

Components and Missions

The Texas State Guard (TXSG) is a branch of the Texas Military Forces. Its function is to provide mission-ready military forces to assist State and local authorities in times of State emergencies. Homeland security and community service are conducted through Defense Support to Civil Authorities (DSCA). The TXSG augments the other two branches of the Texas Military Forces, the Texas Army National Guard, and Texas Air National Guard, as force multipliers. Missions are directed by the Commander-In-Chief (CINC) of the Texas Military Forces, the Governor of Texas. The Texas State Guard is ultimately commanded by the Texas Adjutant General (TAG).

Missions

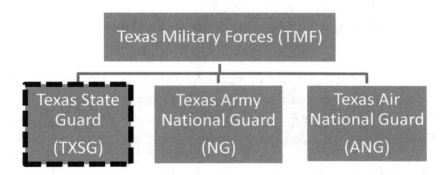

Headquartered at Camp Mabry in Austin, TX, The Adjutant General of the Texas Military Forces is a National Guard (which includes Air National Guard) General.

The Texas State Guard (TXSG) is composed of four volunteer coequal components. They are: (1) **The Medical Brigade**, (2) **Army Component**, (3) **Air Component**, and the (4) **Maritime Regiment**.

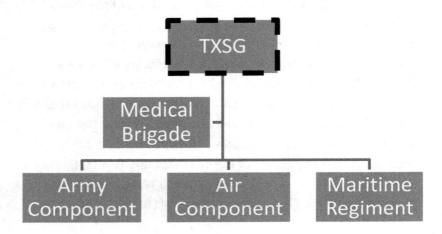

Army - The mission of the Army Component is to provide trained soldiers for Defense Support to Civil Authorities (DSCA), support the Texas Army National Guard, and non-governmental organizations (NGO).

Air - The mission of the Air Component is to provide mission-capable airmen as a force multiplier for the Texas Air National Guard, and for other missions in support of homeland security through Defense Support to Civil Authorities (DSCA).

Maritime - The mission of the Texas Maritime Regiment (TMAR) is to provide highly trained military personnel for Defense Support to Civil Authorities (DSCA), for operations in the maritime, littoral, and riverine environments in support of homeland defense and in response to man-made or natural disasters.

Medical - The mission of the Texas Medical Brigade (TMB) is to augment health and medical support in times of need. TMB maintains a highly trained force that is rapidly deployable to provide appropriately qualified Health, Medical and Support personnel in accordance with the Defense Support of Civil Authorities (DSCA) missions.

Components

A breakdown of the Texas State Guard organizations and units would look like:

TX State Guard Headquarters

Headquarters
Role: Headquarters
Area of Operation: Camp Mabry, Austin, Texas

TX State Guard Units (Army Component)

1st Regiment (The Alamo Guards)
Role: Civil Affairs
Area of Operation: South Texas (San Antonio, Corpus Christi, Westlaco, Zapata)

2nd Regiment (Austin Greys)
Role: Civil Affairs
Area of Operation: Central Texas (Temple, Brownwood, Clifton, Killeen, Waco, Austin)

4th Regiment (Panther City Fencibles)
Role: Civil Affairs
Area of Operation: Northwest/North Central Texas (Fort Worth, Denton, Wichita Falls, Mineral Wells)

8th Regiment (Terry's Texas Rangers)
Role: Civil Affairs
Area of Operation: Southeast Texas (Houston, Bryan, Huntsville, Beaumont, Port Arthur)

19th Regiment (Parson's Brigade)
Role: Civil Affairs
Area of Operation: Northeast/North Central Texas (Dallas, Grand Prarie, Wylie, Kilgore, New Boston)

39th Composite Regiment (Roughnecks)
Role: Civil Affairs / Medical
Area of Operation: West Texas (Lubbock, El Paso, Midland, Amarillo)

Air Component
Role: Support the Texas Air National Guard.
Area of Operation: Statewide
- 4th Air Wing, 417 ASG (San Angelo)
- 4th Air Wing, 436 ASG (Grand Prairie)
- 4th Air Wing, 454 ASG (Dallas)
- 4th Air Wing, 482 ASG (Wichita Falls)
- 5th Air Wing, 401 ASG (Austin)
- 5th Air Wing, 447 ASG (Houston)
- 5th Air Wing, 449 ASG (San Antonio)

*** ASG's refer to "Air Support Groups"

Maritime Regiment (TMAR)
Role: Maritime, littoral, and riverine operations.
Area of Operation: Statewide
- 1st Battalion (Huntsville)
- 2nd Battalion (San Antonio)
- 3rd Battalion (Dallas)
- TMAR Band (Austin/Statewide)

Medical Reserve Corps (Medical Rangers)
Role: Public health emergencies
Area of Operation: Statewide

TXSG Chain-Of-Command & Leadership

[FILL IN]

TXSG Commander-In-Chief / Governor State of Texas

_____

TXSG Vice Commander-In-Chief/Lt Governor State of Texas

_____

Texas Adjutant General (TAG) _____

TXSG Commander _____

Senior Enlisted Advisor _____

TXSG Vice-Commander _____

TXSG (Army Component) Commander

_____

TXSG (Air Component) Commander

_____

TXSG (TMAR Component) Commander

_____

TXSG (Medical Brigade) Commander _____

Public Affairs Officer _____

TXSG Legal/JAG _____

TXSG Chaplain _____

Your Unit Information

Your Unit Name _____

Your Unit Commander _____

Your Unit Vice Commander _____

Your Unit Sr Enlisted Advisor _____

NOTES:

Where Does the TXSG Get Its Authority?

In law, the Texas State Guard is specifically defined as a State Defense Force (SDF), and is the official State militia, as defined by both the Federal, and State Constitutions.

Obviously, Texas had an organized military force prior to becoming part of the United States, and defeating the Mexican military and become an independent Republic. In current law, the Texas State Guard gets its authorities to exist from:

1. Texas Government Codes (Section 437)
2. The US Constitution (Amendment 2)
3. US Code (Title 32)

Laws and Codes

Section 437 of the Texas Government Code states:

"Texas State Guard" means the volunteer military forces that provide community service and emergency response activities for this state, as organized under the Second Amendment to the United States Constitution, and operating as a defense force authorized under 32 U.S.C. Section 109."

Amendment 2, US Constitution

"A well-regulated militia being necessary to the security of a free state, the right of the people to keep and bear arms shall not be infringed."

32 U.S. Code § 109

(c) In addition to its National Guard, if any, a State, the Commonwealth of Puerto Rico, the District of Columbia, Guam, or the Virgin Islands may, as provided by its laws, organize and maintain defense forces. A defense force established under this section may be used within the jurisdiction concerned, as its chief executive (or commanding general in the case of the District of Columbia) considers necessary, but it may not be called, ordered, or drafted into the armed forces.

(d) A member of a defense force established under subsection (c) is not, because of that membership, exempt from service in the armed forces, nor is he entitled to pay, allowances, subsistence, transportation, or medical care or treatment, from funds of the United States.

What is a "State Defense Force"?

State Defense Forces (SDFs) are unique and separate entities from the other branches of the military. They are traditional, direct descendants from America's colonial history, where each township, settlement, or colony had its own volunteers to help protect it from external forces. Today, State Defense Forces are not military branches under the Department of Defense; they are wholly State owned organizations who only work on behalf of the State that has organized them.

Among the many States currently maintaining SDFs along with Texas include:

Alabama, Alaska, California, Connecticut, Georgia, Indiana, Maryland, Massachusetts, Michigan, Mississippi, Missouri, New Mexico, New York, Ohio, Oregon, Puerto Rico, South Carolina, Tennessee, Vermont, Virginia, and Washington.

What are the differences between Federal and State military forces? State Defense forces can NEVER be federalized as per Title 32 of the US Codes. They can never be directly brought under the authority of the Federal Government. In contrast, National Guard personnel may be called up by the Federal Government, and deployed on missions as the Federal Government sees fit.

Whereas the President of the United States is the Commander-In-Chief of the US Military to include the Reserve and National Guard forces, the Commander-In-Chief of State Defense Forces is the Governor of the state whom organized them. Being a solely State entity means that State Defense Forces have certain flexibilities that DoD or Federal forces cannot be flexible on. One of the most basic examples of this includes, Posse Comitatus.

Posse Comitatus is a Latin term that refers to "Community Power" or "Power of a Community". The modern use of this term refers to the Federal Government's (Specifically the US Military's) inability to enforce State Laws. The Posse Comitatus Act (18 June 1878) was enshrined to limit the Federal Government's ability to use military forces to act as Domestic Law Enforcement.

When Does Posse Comitatus Apply?

	Commander-In-Chief	Can Be Federalized	Posse Comitatus
State Defense Forces	Governors	Never	Never
National Guard	Governors OR Presidents	Yes	When Federalized
US Military	President	Always	Under Martial Law
US Reserve	President	Always	Under Martial Law

Why Doesn't Posse Comitatus Apply to The TXSG?

The TXSG does not work on behalf of the Federal Government and is therefore not funded by the Federal Government. As such, it can never be a federal entity enforcing State laws. As a State Force, Posse Comitatus does not apply, except for in appearance. Since TXSG wear the uniforms that the US Military, US Reserve Forces, and/or National Guard (whom can be federalized) wear, we can easily be mistaken by Texans as being a part of the US Military. Therefore **we must ALWAYS identify ourselves as members of the "Texas State Guard"**, and be cognizant that if other Texans see us as Federal Forces, it may lead to an unfortunate confrontation.

Texas, History, and the TXSG

- The "Lone Star State" title is due to the fact that Texas was once an independent Republic/Nation.
- Texas is the largest of the 48 contiguous United States.
- Texas encompases 268,000+ Square Miles.
- Texas has 254 Individual Counties.
- There are 1,215 Texas cities/towns in total.
- Texas is the second most populous State in the US.
- The Capital of Texas is Austin.
- The largest city in Texas is Houston.
- The State Constitution of Texas was adopted in 1876.
- Texas borders the states of; Arkansas, Louisiana, New Mexico, and Oklahoma. Additionally, Texas borders the Country of Mexico.
- Texas borders the Gulf Of Mexico and has 367 miles of Coastline.
- Additionally, Texas has 3750 Streams and 15 Major Rivers.
- There are 130,000,000 acres of Agricultural land.
- Texas encompases 10 Climate Regions.
- Texas climbs from Sea Level to 8000ft.
- Hurricanes regularly engulf on the Gulf Coast.
- The total length of the Texas/Mexico Border is 1,254 miles.
- There are 45 Texas/Mexico Border Crossings.
- Due to tough caliche ground in much of the state, rain waters do not absorb quickly, and flash flooding is a natural occurance.
- Texas is not known for its snowfall, however, the north-western portion of the State, nearest to New Mexico and Colorado regularly see snowfall.
- There are 366,274 miles of pipeline cross Texas.
- Texas has 326 Power Plants that serve her needs.

TXSG Out-Of-State Deployments?

As a Texas State military force, the TXSG does not deploy beyond the border of the State. Exceptions can be made under circumstances where two States coordinate and both State's Governors agree to such deployments. There has only been one time in which this has occurred, that being, Hurricane Katrina in 2005, where Texas State Guardsmen deployed to assist within the State of Louisiana.

History of Texas

Texas has a unique history within the United States. Not only has Texas been under the ownership of the European countries Spain and France, it was also absorbed by Mexico. Additionally, it fought for its independence from Mexico and became its own Republic/Nation prior to becoming part of the United States.

The Texas State Guard's history *IS* the history of the State of Texas. That history extends back to the year 1823 when the Mexican Government allowed Stephen F. Austin (the namesake of Austin, TX) to organize the first non-Mexican military unit serving in its "Tejas" region. The units under Austin maintained peace until all military units/militias came under the command of Sam Houston and the Republic of Texas in 1835.

The Term *Six Flags Over Texas* represents the rich history and traditions of Texas. The six flags represent the national flags that flew over Texas.

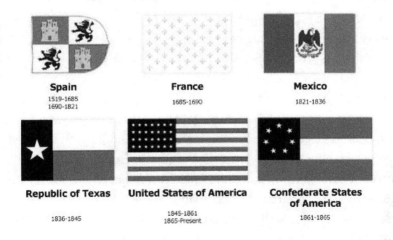

Spain	France	Mexico
1519-1685 1690-1821	1685-1690	1821-1836

Republic of Texas	United States of America	Confederate States of America
1836-1845	1845-1861 1865-Present	1861-1865

The area in which Texas currently resides was previously a part of other nations. Occasionally, Texans might hear Mexican citizens or politicians suggest that Texas used to be part of Mexico. That is true; however, they ignore the fact that Texas (as well as Mexico) used to be part of Spain and France.

Spain: *"New Spain"* (1519-1685)

Spain entered North America in 1519 and named/declared the area it colonized as, New Spain. Spain completed its total conquest of the Aztec Empire in 1521 when they captured the Aztec Emperor, Cuauhtémoc, and conquered the Aztec capital. The King of Spain appointed his leaders (Viceroy) within the region and ruled the area as a Spanish colony. Much of the area that Spain claimed, would later become Mexico.

France: *"French Texas"* (1685-1690)

Colonial rivalry engulfed much of Europe, and would include several North American colonies. The French and Spanish rivalry led them into the Franco-Spanish wars from 1635-1659. The near collapse of Spanish Empire in 1640 led to the end of the myth that Spain was invincible. The *Peace Of The Pyrenees* Treaty was a compromise signed in 1659 between the two empires that ended the war between them. The French took the opportunity to attempt colonies in New Spain (which would become Mexico). In 1684, the French attempted to build a colony in on what is now the Texas coast. By 1690, Fort St. Louis, was a failed colony and was abandoned, and the French withdrew from the area.

Spain: *"Spanish Texas"* (1690-1821)

After the Spanish find the remains of Fort Saint Louis, the Spanish Empire makes a concerted effort to colonize the area to

keep the French away. The Spanish sent several expeditions into the land that would become Texas. Eventually, the Spanish escorted Catholic missionaries into Texas in 1716 and established the first missions including, one in San Antonio. The Spanish would stay firmly in control of Texas in spite of Indian attacks.

Mexico: *"Mexican Texas"* (1821-1836)

Mexico Declared independence from Spain on 16 September 1810. After defending their independence from Spain for 11 years, Mexico secured its independence. The Mexican War of Independence forced Spain to evacuate the area. The Mexican Empire was the first independent  state of Mexico after the Spanish empire. It lasted from 1821, until 1823. Mexico became a Federal Republic in 1824, after the Mexican Emperor abdicated power. The Federal Republic fought off several recolonization attempts by Spain until it was recognized by Spain as an independent nation in 1836. Texas would become a province of the NEW nation of Mexico.

Texas Rising

Mexico fought and won its independence from Spain, in the exact same fashion that Texas would fight for its independence from Mexico. After many "Americans" continued to immigrate into Tejas, a Mexican Province, the Mexican government had enough and on April 6th of 1830, forbid any more "Texians" from moving into the Tejas region. Anger seeped up and the Mexican military attempted to stop people from moving into the territory through taxation and property rights law.

> **"Tejanos"** were pioneers from the Spanish Colonial period or those who descended from Spanish Mexicans.

> **"Texians"** were the non-Hispanic residents of Mexico prior to the Republic Of Texas.

Texians asked for reforms regarding Texas, and the Mexican government refused. On 26 June 1832, the first casualties occurred between those living in Tejas and the Mexican government during the Battle of Velasco. Texians attacked the Mexicans at Camp Velasco. They won after the Mexican Commander surrendered after running out of ammunition.

NOTE: "Tejas" originated from the Caddo Indians name "Tay-yas" (friend), one of the states of the United Mexican States. The name would later become pronounced "Texas" by those who entered the area.

From 1833 to 1834, Mexico continued to refuse any change in policy towards Texas and would eventually arrest Stephen Austin, further angering the Texians.

After refusing to surrender a cannon back to the Mexican Army and defiantly telling them to "Come And Take It", on 2 October 1835, the Battle Of Gonzales erupts and the War Of Texas Independence begins. The Gonzales Flag is born.

1835 - On 9 October, The Battle Of Goliad erupts and the Texans win. On 28 October, the Battle Of Concepcion begins and Texans are outnumbered 5-to-1, but still win decisively.

1835 - The government of Texas decreed a Militia on 27 November

1835 - 11 December, The Texians capture San Antonio.

1836 - On 23 February, the Alamo is under siege by 5000 Mexican soldiers. They are commanded by the Mexican General Santa Anna de Lopez.

1836 - On 1 March, Texans have a Constitutional Convention and form a new government. On 2 March, the Texas Declaration of Independence is adopted. The Mexican Government is angered. On 6 March, The Alamo, in San Antonio is lost. 187 Texians are killed, or executed.

1836 - On 27 March, Santa Anna ordered the execution of Texans during the Goliad Massacre. When other Texans hear about the massacre, they become infuriated. The rallying cry of Texas Independence becomes, "Remember The Alamo", and "Remember Goliad."

Texas: *"Republic of Texas"* (1836-1845)

On 21 April of 1836, forces of Sam Houston catch up to and decisively defeats General Santa Anna's forces during the Battle of San Jacinto. It becomes one of the most decisive victories in military history. It was:

Mexico	Texians
650 Killed	11 killed
208 Wounded	30 Wounded
300 Captured	0 Captured – THEY WON

The Republic of Texas is born. Texas would begin to grow as a separate country, to include Embassies in Paris and London.

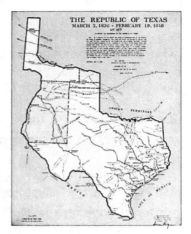

The border and property of the Republic Of Texas used to extend into modern Oklahoma, Kansas, Colorado, and New Mexico.

1836 - The Republic of Texas government continued the Militia authorization in 6 December.

As the Texas Republic won its independence, the "Militia" became the "Army of the Republic Of Texas." The name changed, but a majority of the people stayed the same.

The United States of America: *"Statehood"* (1845-1861)

Texas is unique amongst other states within the United States. It was a Republic that fought for its own independence and Texans **VOTED** to join the United States. Unlike other states, it was NOT conquered, annexed, seized, or purchased from another nation.

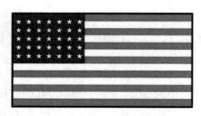

Texas held a convention to join the Union on 4 July 1845. President of the United States, James K. Polk, offered to buy New Mexico and California, but the Mexican Government was offended. Mexico prepared for war, and President Polk sent US Military forces into Texas and had small skirmishes with the Mexican Military. The United States Declared war with Mexico, and the United States sent military personnel into Mexico City and occupied it.

The Treaty of Guadalupe Hidalgo was signed in 1848. Mexico was paid $15 Million for much of the current Southern border.

Confederate States of America: *"Civil War Era"* (1861-1865)

Under the Auspices of State's Rights and Slavery, Texan politicians, industry, and agricultural leaders lead a movement of secession from the United States. Under a referendum, Texans voted to leave the union and joined the Confederate States Of America (CSA) leading to the Civil War.

Sam Houston rejected Texas Secession and was deposed from his position as Governor after he refused to pledge allegiance to the Confederacy. Over 70,000 Texans served in the Confederate Army and Texans fought in every major battle throughout the war. On 2 June 1865, a formal surrender ended the Confederacy.

United States of America: *"Reconstruction"* (1865-Present)

After the Civil War, the Confederate States of America was gone, and a period of Reconstruction began.

1870 - Two branches of Militia were codified in law. The Reserve-Militia, and the Active-Militia together become known as the "State Guard," and they begin operations as the Texas State Guard on 1 January.

1903 - The Dick Act (or Militia Act) separated a "National Guard" from a "Reserve Militia" (State Guard) and spelled-out when State military units could be federalized. "State Guard" units would become "National Guard" units as Congress attempted to regulate the qualifications and standards of the different state militias and military units across the US, to allow an overall Commander more control of how the units would, and could fight in future conflicts.

"Militia" and the Texas State Guard

The TX State Guard is a "Militia", in exactly the same way as the Texas National Guard, or Air National Guard are. The National Guard and the State Guard both have the same legal lineage, beginning with the Militia Act of 1903.

The word "*Militia*" has become a charged word with negative connotations associated to it. It is important to watch how you use that term based upon your audience. When a modern organization is labeled a militia in modern English usage, it is usually to define that organization as; secessionist, violent, counter-law, conspiratorial, or as an otherwise anti-government group of people.

The Texas State Guard has a history that extends to when the word "Militia" was positive, honorable, and represented the best values in Texan and American societies, to include, volunteerism patriotism, and dedication.

World War 1

During World War I, Congress authorized the states to maintain Home Guards, which were reserve forces outside the Reserve Guard forces that were then being deployed by the Federal Government as part of the National Army. The Secretary of War was authorized to furnish these Home Guard units with rifles, ammunition, and supplies. Texas Reserve Guard was issued Rifles, Shotguns, Machine Guns, and Vehicles.

World War 2

World War 2 had been initiated in 1939 and the US had managed to stay out of conflict. But was supporting the United Kingdom and France. It was apparent that war was coming. In 1940, the National Defense act of 1916 was amended and authorizing the states to maintain "military forces other than National Guard", even though states were already doing so. Additionally, it authorized the War Department to train and arm these new state forces that would come to be known as "State Defense Guards."

1941 - The Adjutant General of Texas organized 50 Battalions of the Texas Defense Guard after the Texas Legislature passed its Defense Act, and the Governor signed it in February 1941.

1941 - In July, The United States War Department issued Rifles, Machine Guns, Searchlights, Uniforms, Sirens, and military vehicles to Texas, and other States, for the Defense Guard's Use.

1941 - December 7th; Japan attacked the US at Pearl Harbor

1943 - The "Texas Defense Guard" officially became renamed back to "Texas State Guard".

Modern Era TXSG Deployments

The TXSG lineage extends back to the origins of our State. The Modern Era, would include numerous deployments and activations to assist the State of Texas in  maintaining a lasting peace and order. The first activation of the modern Texas State Guard was the Beaumont Race Riots of 1943.

Beaumont Race Riots of 1943

The Beaumont Race Riots of 1943 serve as the first test of the Texas State Guard after the War Department issued Rifles to State Defense Forces in 1941. Sparked by rape allegations, Shipyard workers attempted to lynch an individual. The Sheriff stopped the attempt, however, riots spread across the town. Several black-owned businesses were burned down.

The Mayor of Beaumont, TX asked the Governor to declare Martial Law and sent in the Texas State Guard. The TXSG quickly had more than 2200 armed personnel in  Beaumont the following morning. The city was secured and tensions were calmed. TXSG Personnel worked closely with police and assisted in foot patrols. They even assisted Firefighters in putting out fires. Overall, two people were killed, and over 50 were injured in the riots. The riots were ended largely because of the decisive TXSG presence.

TXSG Members helping extinguish a business fire

TXSG Member on patrol with local Police

1947 - The Texas State Guard decreased in size at the end of World War II. It wouldn't be used in any large measure until April of 1947 when a freighter and fertilizer plant exploded, killing 580+ people, and injuring nearly 4000 others in the port of Texas City, TX in Galveston County. In July, the TXSG was disbanded after the Federal Government ended the legal athority for States to have military forces expired. But Texans did not agree. They did not disband the Texas State Guard in direct defiance of the Federal Government. Instead, they authorized a "State Reserve Corps" for the next decade.

1948 - The Texas Military Reserve Corps was activated by the State and became active. They utilized all the same equipment, had the same people, and continued just as the Texas State Guard; but with a different name.

In October, the First Naval Battalion was started and the Sumoria was commissioned as the flagship of Texas by Governor Beauford. The 60-foot long ship was used for training purposes along with, the then retired, Battleship U.S.S. Texas. The Sumoria's first Skipper; was the boat's owner, Sterling Hogan.

1955 - Congress began to understand and accept that the States would continue to have their own military forces, in spite of the wishes of the Federal Government, and reauthorized the many State's authority to "legalize" them.

1965 - Ten years after the Federal reauthorization; on 30 August, the Texas Reserve Corps was ended, and returned back to being the "Texas State Guard". With the same units, leadership, and equipment.

The TX State Guard has gotten more complex, has integrated more into the TX Military Forces, and grown as need has arisen. A separate Air Wing was organized in 1996; the 4th Air Wing. A Medical Brigade was organized in 2003. The Maritime Regiment (TMAR), was stood up in 2006. The Air Wing would become a separate component of the Texas State Guard in 2006, where it was under the Army Component prior to that.

Although not a complete list, the following represents a sampling of modern-era Texas **State Guard Activations**: through 2015. 2016 saw were several activations for training missions, as well, as for significant flooding events.

Partial List of Texas State Guard Activations	
Riots Beaumont	1943
Texas City Storms	1943
Texas City Explosions	1947
Alice City Floods	1951
Guadalupe River Floods, Victoria	1951
Tank Fire, corpus Christi	1952
Hurricane Alice, Rio Grande Valley	1954
Victoria Flooding	1956
Dallas Tornado	1957
Hurricane Audrey, Orange and La.	1957
Edinburgh & Rio Grande City Flooding	1958
Tanker Fire, Houston	1959
49th AD Div Activation	1961
Midland TX Storm	1966
Lubbock Tornado	1970
Zapata Tornado	1970
Bishop Tornado	1970
Hurricane Cecilia, Corpus Christi	1970
Hurricane Fern, Gulf Coast	1971
Luling Train Wreck	1971
New Braunfels Flooding	1971

Pasadena Pipeline Rupture	1972
Dallas Riots	1973
Burnet & Hubbard Tornados	1973
Tropical Storm Delia, Gulf Coast	1973
Lake Worth and Nacadocias Flooding	1974
Anthony Fires	1974
Anthrax Quarantine, Gratesville	1974
Refugio flooding	1974
Trickham & Coleman Tornadoes	1975
Baytown & Pasadena Flooding	1975
Galena Park Elevator Explosion	1976
Hurricane Anita, McAllen	1977
Tropical Storm Amelia, Kerrville	1978
Wichita Falls & Vernon Tornados	1979
Hurricane Allen, Gulf Coast	1980
President Reagan Texas Visit	1983
Texas Sesquicentennial	1985
Papal Visit, San Antonio	1987
Abilene Ice Storm	1987
Marshall Train Derailment	1987
Midland Power Outage	1990
Lackland Air Force Base, Gulf War Perimeter Security	1990
DFW Tornados	1994
Tropical Storm Bonnie, Pasadena	1999
San Antonio & New Braunfels, Brownwood	2002
Space Shuttle Colombia (STS-107) Search, Security, and Recovery	2003
Hurricane Ivan	2005
Hurricane Katrina	2005
Hurricane Rita	2005
Operation Wrangler	2006
Marble Falls Flood	2007
Lake Leon Flood	2007

Hurricane Dean	2007
Hurricane Dolly	2008
Hurricane Gustav	2008
Hurricane Ike	2008
Operation Border Star	2009
Bastrop Wildfires	2011
Operation Final Rest	2014
Operation Strong Safety	2014
Operation Secure Texas	2015
Central Texas Floods	2015

Ongoing/ Current Operations

Along with the historic deployments and operations, the Texas State Guard also assists in yearly programs and ongoing projects for the State of Texas. These programs assist the State Of Texas and directly benefit Texans. Some of these include:

- Military Ceremonies & Funeral Support
- Operation Border Star
- Operation Lone Star
- Oral Rabies Vaccination Program
- Support to State Operations Center (SOC)

The Texas State Guard conducts numerous military ceremonies, supports military funerals, and participates in parades throughout Texas.

Operation Border Star (OBS)

Operation Border Star is a long-running operation. It involves assisting and coordinating information between State and Federal Agencies in support of Border Operations. Texas State Guard works under the Texas Department of Public Safety- Texas Ranger Division. Those selected to work in Joint Operations Intelligence Centers, or (JOICs). The JOICs are located in Border Patrol, or Local Police facilities. It is a full time, competitively paid, job for Texas State Guard members selected to fill a position.

Operation Lone Star (OLS)

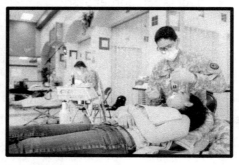

Operation Lone Star is a Yearly Humanitarian deployment conducted on the southern border to assist those who cannot afford medical attention, with receiving basic medical services from TXSG and State of Texas medical professionals. This is a Medical Brigade mission and they see over 5000 individuals per event.

Oral Rabies Vaccination (ORV)

The Oral Rabies Vaccination Program is the dropping of Rabies Vaccine (within meat/bait) into the woods from aircraft. The foxes, feral cats, and rodents, consume the bait and this helps in limiting the number of animals that contract Rabies.

SOC and BSOC

Additionally, the TXSG assists in operating the Texas *State Operations Center (SOC)*, and the *Border Security Operations Center (BSOC)*. Both Centers have members assigned to various full-time State of Texas positions. Headquartered in Austin, TX, These Operations Centers serve

as focal points for information and intelligence during incidents, emergencies, or Border Related crime and information.

TXSG Rank Structures

Historically, Texas State Military forces have used multiple rank structures, including presumably, the Mexican rank structure used when the Mexican Government allowed Stephen Austin to create militia units within the Tejas Region (the area that would become Texas). As Texas became independent, The TXSG has mirrored the Rank Structure of the US Military.

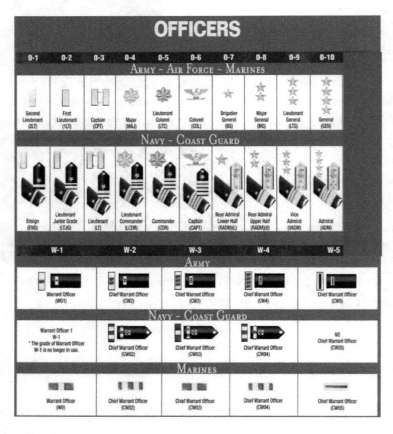

ENLISTED

	E-1	E-2	E-3	E-4	E-5	E-6	E-7	E-8	E-9

Army

no insignia			Corporal (CPL)						
	Private E-1 (PV1)	Private E-2 (PV2)	Private First Class (PFC)	Specialist (SPC)	Sergeant (SGT)	Staff Sergeant (SSG)	Sergeant First Class (SFC)	Master Sergeant (MSG) / First Sergeant (1SG)	Sergeant Major (SGM) / Command Sergeant Major (CSM)

Marines

no insignia									
	Private (Pvt)	Private First (PFC)	Lance Corporal (LCpl)	Corporal (Cpl)	Sergeant (Sgt)	Staff Sergeant (SSgt)	Gunnery Sergeant (GySgt)	Master Sergeant (MSgt) / First Sergeant (1stSgt)	Master Gunnery Sergeant (MGySgt) / Sergeant Major (SgtMaj)

Air Force

no insignia									
	Airman Basic (AB)	Airman (Amn)	Airman First Class (A1C)	Senior Airman (SrA)	Staff Sergeant (SSgt)	Technical Sergeant (TSgt)	Master Sergeant (MSgt) / First Sergeant (E-7)	Senior Master Sergeant (SMSgt) / First Sergeant (E-8)	Chief Master Sergeant (CMSgt) / First Sergeant (E-9) / Command Chief Master Sergeant (CCM)

Navy

no insignia									
	Seaman Recruit (SR)	Seaman Apprentice (SA)	Seaman (SN)	Petty Officer Third Class (PO3)	Petty Officer Second Class (PO2)	Petty Officer First Class (PO1)	Chief Petty Officer (CPO)	Senior Chief Petty Officer (SCPO)	Master Chief Petty Officer (MCPO) / Force or Fleet Command Master Chief Petty Officer (FORMC)(FLTMC)

Coast Guard

	Seaman Recruit (SR)	Seaman Apprentice (SA)	Seaman (SN)	Petty Officer Third Class (PO3)	Petty Officer Second Class (PO2)	Petty Officer First Class (PO1)	Chief Petty Officer (CPO)	Senior Chief Petty Officer (SCPO)	Master Chief Petty Officer (MCPO) / Command Master Chief (CMC)

The TXSG currently utilizes components of all five Federal rank structures and specialty badges, due to the backgrounds of the personnel who have entered the TXSG from the Department Of Defense. These include the Army, Navy/Coast Guard, Marine Corps, and Air Force.

Staff System

While working with TXSG personnel, you may hear someone referred to as "N1", or "S1". These terms reference the General Staff System (or Continental Staff System). They are a means of organizing functions of the personnel within a unit that comply with the units of other similar, or even dissimilar, military organizations. When organized in this system a British military Officer, can contact a US or French military unit and find the individual he may need during a joint operation.

1	Manpower / Personnel
2	Intelligence / Security
3	Operations
4	Logistics
5	Plans
6	Communications / Signal
7	Training
8	Finance
9	Civil Affairs

The TXSG utilizes this system to work within TXSG components, or even National Guard units with whom we are working alongside.

A – Staff | Air Component   (Example "A-6" – Communication)

S – Staff | Army Component   (Example "S-3" – Operations)

N – Staff | Maritime Component (Example "N-1" – Personnel)

J – Staff | Texas State Guard HQ (Example "J-1" – Personnel)

G – Staff | Texas Military Forces HQ (Example "G-1" Personnel)

Dress and Appearance

When people come in contact with you while you are in uniform, they are not only judging you, but they are judging the Texas State Guard as an organization that would have you within it. It is important that all of us always act appropriately and are perceived as professional. Dress and appearance are an important means to improve TXSG goals, and maintain professionalism.

Shaving & Hair

Always ensure that you are clean shaven, including any beards or mustaches. Your haircut should be trimmed and intentional. Refer to your component's (Army, Air, TMAR) specific regulations for specific information. These regulations normally mirror whichever DoD regulation your component is traditionally based.

Refer to the US military Dress and Appearance standard regarding the uniform you wear within the TXSG. It is not possible to comply with the Army, Air Force, Navy, or Marine Corps standards of uniform wear, and not comply with the TXSG Standard.

Uniform and Boot Maintenance

Your uniform should be kept clean, dry, and serviceable at a minimum and pressed at best. In the TXSG there are no rules against ironing your uniform. But always follow proper instructions regarding care of your uniform. There is no reason for our uniforms to appear wrinkled or disheveled.

Modern military boots are extremely simple to maintain. A damp washcloth, with a tiny bit of dish soap or shampoo scrubbed on the suede, and around the sole of the boot should do the job.

Activation

Ready Bag

Although Texas has been lucky regarding Hurricanes in the past decade, TXSG Members must always be prepared to serve on short notice. This preparation includes having a packed activation ready bag packed during Hurricane season. Plan on being in the field for 72 hours without resupply. Bring emergency cash (at least $20 in small bills or coins). Do not depend on credit cards or checks and do not anticipate receiving change for large bills. Pack all items in an easy to carry duffle bag or back pack.

Uniform:

2 - Uniforms and accessory items suitable for the climate
1 - Pair of Boots to match uniform
2 - Field headgear to match uniform
1 - Multi-purpose knife (Leatherman style tool)
1 - Personal identification (TX DL, ID tags, blood type tapes, TXSG ID Card and orders)

Personal Equipment:

1 - Full brim hardhat or helmet
2 - Changes of undergarments (underwear, t-shirts, and socks)
1 - Bathing Suit
1 - Shower Shoes
1 - Watch
1 - Flashlight (w/ spare batteries)
2 - Black ball-point pens

2 - Black sharpies
1 - Note pad
1 - Poncho/wet weather gear
1 - Pair of leather palm work gloves
1 - Safety glasses
1 - Spare eyeglasses (if worn)
1 - Sun glasses (UV protection)
1 - Field Expedient First Aid kit
1 - Insect repellant
1 - Lip balm with sun screen
1 - Sunscreen lotion
1 - Butane lighter/waterproof matches in sealed container
2 - Water containers (full) w/holders (1 quart/liter in size)
1 - Sleeping bag or poncho liner
1 - Bath towel
1 - Personal care pack (soap, razor, toothpaste, toothbrush, deodorant, and prescription medicines)
1 - Roll of Duct Tape
1 - Roll of toilet paper
3 - Power or Granola Bars
1 - MRE (Meals Ready to Eat)

Optional Items

- Tools to do your (and your unit's) particular TXSG function
- Laptop/Tablet/iPad and Charger
- Cell Phone and Charger
- Load Carrying Equipment
- Cot
- Sewing Kit
- Waterproof bag
- Whistle with Lanyard

Field Hygiene

When deployed, Texas State Guard Members tend to get involved and stay involved. The tendency to work long hours should not stop us from taking care of ourselves. Sometimes showers and bathrooms are not available, however, there are common-sense actions that can be taken to ensure you maintain your ability to operate, as well as, to maintain your health. Some of these actions would include:

> - Keep as clean as you can. As a minimum, bathe feet, hands and private parts. If possible, change your underwear and socks regularly (goes without saying).
> - Have a short, regulation haircut, and keep your fingernails short and clean.
> - If you cannot wash your uniform, crumple it, shake it out, and hang it outside in the sun, turned inside out, for at least two hours. Military Uniforms are low-maintenance.
> - Get out of wet clothing a quickly as you can. This is particularly important during cold-weather operations.
> - Inspect your body frequently for "critters", such as ticks, spiders, or other disease carrying insects.
> - Take care of your feet. This means properly fitted boots and socks, daily washing, toenails trimmed, straight across, use shower shoes when in garrison (using public showers), and take immediate and proper care of blisters and corns.
> - Brush teeth at least once (or thrice) daily. Be courteous to others.
> - Regard every water source as contaminated until you know otherwise. Drink only water which has been purified.

➢ Drink plenty of water but do not drink large amounts at one time. In warm weather, increase your intake of salt.
➢ Keep your mess gear scrupulously clean. Wash mess gear in hot, soapy water, and rinse it in boiling water, before and after each meal. Be sure no garbage, grease or food particles adhere to mess gear between meals.
➢ Carry toilet paper and keep it dry. Relieve yourself only in the appropriate, designated area.
➢ Avoid direct contact with damp ground, especially when hot or perspiring. Likewise avoid drafts (If possible).
➢ Use mosquito net and keep it in good condition (if necessary and when available).

NOTES:

Force Protection and Anti-Terrorism

Force Protection and Anti-Terrorism are becoming more and more important to the Texas State Guard, our personnel, and the success of our missions. Paying attention to Force Protection and following good Anti-Terrorism practices are the responsibility of EVERY Texas State Guard Member. There is nothing more important in the security, of our members, families, units, and our Texas communities.

> Force Protection:
>
> *Actions taken to prevent or mitigate hostile, or non-hostile actions against TXSG personnel.*

Anti-Terrorism (AT), focuses on threats from terrorism, and terrorists. It is not to be confused with the *offensive* actions actively used to engage (kill) Terrorists, Counter-Terrorism. Anti-Terrorism is everyone's responsibility and is defined as:

> Anti-Terrorism:
>
> *Defensive "program" used to reduce the vulnerability of TXSG members and property to* terrorist *acts.*

Force Protection Conditions (FPCONs)

The Department of Defense utilizes a grading system to identify the 5 Force Protection Conditions. Each condition can be raised or lowered by the Chain of Command, depending on intelligence, threats, or perceived threats to Texas Military Forces personnel.

Condition	Application	Considerations
FPCON NORMAL	Applies when a general global threat of possible terrorist activity exists.	Warrants a routine security posture.
FPCON ALPHA	Applies when there is an increased general threat of possible terrorist activity against personnel or facilities, the nature, and extent of which are unpredictable.	ALPHA measures must be capable of being maintained indefinitely.
FPCON BRAVO	Applies when an increased or more predictable threat of terrorist activity exists.	Sustaining BRAVO measures for a prolonged period may affect operational capability and relations with local authorities.
FPCON CHARLIE	Applies when an incident occurs or intelligence is received indicating some form of terrorist action or targeting against personnel or facilities is likely.	Implementation of CHARLIE measures will create hardship and affect the activities of the unit and its personnel.
FPCON DELTA	Applies in the immediate area where a terrorist attack has occurred or when intelligence has been received that terrorist action against a specific location or person is imminent.	Normally, this FPCON is declared as a localized condition. FPCON DELTA measures are not intended to be sustained for substantial periods.

Targeting the TXSG

Although TXSG members are not "specifically" targeted as citizens of the State of Texas, the uniforms we wear, are those that United States military services and National Guard wear. Those who might attack, or otherwise target the DoD, may unintentionally attack us because we wear the same uniforms. They may not know, nor understand the difference, **AND** they simply may not care that we serve the State of Texas, and not the US Department of Defense. Regardless, it is our responsibility to take actions to protect ourselves. Some of these common sense actions might include:

Watch your Profile and be Unpredictable

- ✓ Dress in a manner as to not attract attention.
- ✓ Blend in to the population around you.
- ✓ Avoid publicity, large crowds, demonstrations, and/or civil disturbances.
- ✓ Vary your routes, times, and modes of travel.
- ✓ Let others know where you're going, and when you plan to return.

Be Alert

- ➢ Watch for anything suspicious, or out of place.
- ➢ If you think/believe you're being followed, go to a Police Station or collect as much information as possible without adding unnecessary risk.
- ➢ Let someone know, if you think you were followed (even with a text message and description)
- ➢ Remain as calm as possible… and think.

If you see something unfamiliar or that causes concern, immediately inform those around you and inform you Chain of Command to any possible threats. ALWAYS Err on the side of caution to any threats.

Texas Department Public Safety, Anti-Terrorism Hotline

Email: txdpsintelcenter@dps.texas.gov

Web Form: https://iwatchx.org

Shelter Operations

Shelter Ops is one of the specific tasks directed to the Texas State Guard by TXSG leadership as one of the primary functions that TXSG Personnel assists our communities with during local emergencies. ***THIS SECTION IS ADDITIONAL INFORMATION THAT IS NOT TAUGHT IN THE TXSG REQUIRED SHELTER FUNDAMENTALS COURSE, BUT ARE HELPFUL REMINDERS WHEN OPERATING IN A SHELTER ENVIRONMENT.***

After a community is ravaged by a natural disaster or Homeland Security incidents, there may come a need to provide assistance to those citizens who find themselves displaced due to the incident.  Shelters may become necessary. High-School gymnasiums, Convention centers or other suitable spaces may become make-shift living quarters. Always Remember:

- Those in shelters, have not chosen to be there.
- They are likely going through an extremely traumatic time in their lives. BE PATIENT.
- They may have lost contact with family, friends, as well as their spouses.
- Some may have lost their homes and everything they own.
- Many may not feel safe around so many strangers.
- Always remain in contact with other TXSG personnel.

Shelter Safety

TXSG members are not Police. It is our duty to inform Law Enforcement to any unsafe conditions within the shelter:

1. Suspicious individuals (criminals, unstable persons)
2. Dangerous living conditions (such as electric wires in water)
3. Strange or odd circumstances
4. Unsafe areas of the shelter (no lighting)
5. Criminal activities (drug use, prostitution)

Personal Safety

Whenever you put too many people in close confines, especially after they may have lost everything, you are inviting turmoil, trouble, and conflict. Shelters that are run with fewer resources than they require are even more likely to breed chaos. Your personal safety, the safety of all the others operating the shelter, as well as the persons living in the shelter, may be in jeopardy. There are some steps that can be taken to increase safety:

- Maintain Cleanliness of the shelter – This ensures people do not feel as though they are sleeping in filth. Ensure there are clean restrooms and plenty of trash cans.
- Section off areas – and limit those areas to personnel who are staying there. Ensure aisles are as wide as possible and color code each area to ensure people can distinguish where they are.
- Give regular briefings to those regarding the shelter
- Never interject yourself into a physical confrontation until law enforcement arrives, and only when directed to do so. Always pay attention to where other TXSG personnel are.

Conflict Resolution in the Shelter

After displaced persons spend uncomfortable periods within a shelter, the opportunity for individuals to become upset or angry with each other increases. Conflicts may naturally arise. It is a duty for TXSG Members to observe and to assist in maintaining peace BEFORE conflict turns dangerous, and civil law enforcement personnel are required. Knowledge and patience increase the odds of avoiding conflict.

The goal of resolving conflicts is: To Gain Voluntary Compliance. Speak to individuals as though they are important. Pay attention to the individual's body language, and pay even greater attention to your own. If you look aggressive, an individual may believe you are physically challenging him, and become physically aggressive. Use patience.

When Communicating

When you are speaking to an individual an elaborate process is being undertaken. Communication is a continuous process of encoding, transmitting, and decoding. Be cognizant, take your time and listen closely when communicating to others. Recognize that the words you choose, your body language, and how the individual you are speaking to can easily be misunderstood. Be patient and understand that the message you are attempting to send could easily become misunderstood by the person you are tempting to communicate with. Especially, when either party is under stress.

The Media and the Public

The Media

There may be times where the Texas State Guard may be in a newspaper or receives some news coverage. Because of this possibility, when we are conducting operations, and are asked questions by reporters, we must always be prepared.

It is not generally a TXSG members' function to answer questions. It is a general rule to forward all questions to the Public Affairs representative for the unit. If you are not aware of whom the Public Affairs representative is, just say politely:

"Let me refer you to my supervisor or a public affairs Officer."

And politely refer them to your Chain-of-Command. Avoid answering questions if you are uncomfortable as a public speaker. Cameras and a microphone in your face can be intimidating AND once, you open the door and answer one question, it will usually lead to a second, third, and more. You might find yourself in an awkward position if you attempt to flee or run from the media.

You may answer simple questions while you are on the move to ensure you're not being seen as rude. As an example; if you are handing out water and are asked by a reporter, or other media a simple question such as;

(Question) *"How much water have you given out?"*
(Answer) *"10-20 Cases"*

You may answer simple, basic questions. Not asking, "How are you?" will come off rude. But, you should avoid all questions when your answer is likely to speak for the TXSG as a whole.

TXSG Member's Role:

- ❖ Contact your Commander or your unit Public Affairs Representative if you feel uncomfortable.
- ❖ Do not give out information regarding activities of your unit that may place them in jeopardy.

Understand and accept that the Media is providing information to citizens/Texans, and that is critical in a free nation. Speaking to the media, answering questions, and taking pictures for, or with, the public is vital in building/maintaining trust to Texans. Media is the primary method that this is accomplished.

[Fill in]
Unit Public Affairs Rep _____
Alternate PA Rep _____

It is our duty to help foster an atmosphere of trust, cooperation, and mutual respect for the working needs of the news media and the TXSG. A positive relationship is a vital goal of the news, and media relations. Be respectful to the media and understand that they are attempting to complete a job, just as we are.

The Public

We Are Texans! And it should go without saying that the entire reason the TXSG survives is to serve the State of Texas and Texans.

It is imperative that we treat Texans as though they are our bosses, because they are our bosses. We must ensure that we support them and maintain our professionalism when they are concerned. Whether at an Airshow, a shelter, or on the street, our job is to maintain our composure and realize that we represent the State of Texas and treat Texans with the utmost courtesy and respect.

What NOT to do when dealing with the media OR the public:

- NEVER get into public arguments... You will be recorded
- NEVER tell lies... You will be a recorded liar.
- NEVER say, "No Comment". You'll look guilty or sneaky
- Avoid using Jargon or Acronyms.

Contact with Foreign Nationals

If you ever have any contact with foreigners (of the US) and they seem to be attempting to gather information about TXSG operations, be calm, patient, and friendly. Contact your Unit Commander, via your chain of command so they can take actions they deem necessary, if any.

Responsibilities of Social Media

Social Media websites such as Facebook, Twitter, Myspace, Vine, and others allow people to share lots of information with lots of people at any given moment. It is important to be careful what information is put on the internet because that allows others to know information that you might not need them to know. To keep ourselves, and our families' safe, we follow some basic rules to protect TXSG members and operations. Members must ALWAYS:

- Pay attention to what you post online.
- Do not click links to visit sites; Type their name into your browser.
- Recognize that everything you post on-line is there to stay. It is permanent.
- Avoid sharing your personal details.

Social media can be a great tool for TXSG units, however, there are certain rules we must follow when using Social Media accounts. It is important that we understand that ANYTHING posted on a TXSG social media site, becomes a statement *OF* the Texas State Guard. Only post professional items, that are NON-POLITICAL in nature.

Remember that if you post pictures of yourself in uniform on your personal web pages or social media, your messages may be accepted as approved by the TXSG. This conflicts with TXSG policy.

Personal Politics

Many of us are proud Texans, and enjoy our freedoms and liberty, however, we must be careful that we do not show contempt for the Federal Government. Although it MAY not be a CRIME for us to express our beliefs (as it is for the National Guard, or DoD), our written or spoken statements may exclude us from serving within the Texas State Guard.

As an inalienable Right, we could not surrender, or give away our rights, even if we wanted do. But we must understand that as a member of a volunteer organization, that organization also gets to express itself as it chooses. It is prudent to avoid issues related to:

- Gun Control
- Concealed Carry
- Homosexuality
- Religion
- Politics

Although, the majority of TXSG members see these issues somewhat similarly, and they have not been an organizational issue for us in our past, these are not issues the TXSG represents publically. Each of us individually, and the TXSG as an entity, must always evaluate whether or not we will be affiliated with each other. If personnel do not represent TXSG values, the TXSG may remove members with little, to no, warning.

TO CLARIFY: Always be careful when you represent yourself as a member of the TXSG. If you are not attentive, your words, thoughts, and ideals may become associated with the TXSG. The TXSG has the final say in whether or not to end its relationship with any member that runs afoul of TXSG, Texas Military Forces, or State Of Texas, Social Media policy.

Texas Department of Public Safety

TXSG does not work alone, we work with, and through, local communities. We depend upon State personnel for our safety

as well. When conducting operations within a community, it is important to be aware of any local law enforcement agencies within the jurisdiction. They will likely be responsible to respond in the case of any emergency, and take action to keep TXSG members safe. Be aware of the local Department of Public Safety (DPS) Offices, and contact numbers if activated. Common STATEWIDE contact information includes:

Emergency Assistance	911
Crime Stoppers	(800) 252-TIPS (8477)
Roadside Assistance	(800) 525-5555
Austin Headquarters	(512) 424-2000
Texas Rangers	(512) 424-2160
Texas Highway Patrol	(512) 506-2847

Street Address:	Texas Department of Public Safety 5805 North Lamar Blvd. Austin, Texas 78752-4431

Emergency Management

Emergency Management is always difficult. The Texas State Guard ASSISTS the State and Counties, in managing emergencies. The Texas State Guard, nor any component in the Texas Military Forces has the authority to seize power from the civilian leadership during an Emergency. **Texas County Judges have that sole responsibility.** They generally appoint Emergency Managers; however, all choices and actions are at their discretion and THEY HAVE THE FINAL WORD. It is important to note that ALL EMERGENCIES ARE LOCAL. Not even in incidents such as, the attacks of 11 September 2001, did the State in which the incident occur, lose control over its responsibility to manage the incident.

> The TXSG (as well as the Army and Air National Guard) is tasked to ASSIST local communities in cases of emergency. NO MORE, NO LESS!

When responding to Emergencies, the TXSG must be trained and prepared to understand the language used by all of the other responders. Nationwide, that language is **"NIMS"** and **"ICS"**.

National Incident Management System (NIMS)

The National Incident Management System (NIMS) is a systematic, proactive approach to guide departments and agencies at all levels of government, nongovernmental organizations, and the private sector to work together seamlessly and manage incidents involving all threats and hazards—regardless of cause, size, location, or complexity—in order to reduce loss of life, property and harm to the environment. The NIMS is the essential foundation to the National Preparedness System (NPS) and provides the template for the management of incidents and operations in support of all five National Planning Frameworks.

NIMS was developed so responders from different jurisdictions and disciplines can work together better to respond to natural disasters and emergencies, including acts of terrorism. NIMS uses a systematic approach to integrate the best existing processes and methods into a unified national framework for incident management, including the five Homeland Security activities.

1. Prevention
2. Protection
3. Response
4. Mitigation
5. Recovery

Incidents typically begin and end locally, and they are managed daily at the lowest possible geographical, organizational, and jurisdictional level. There are other instances where success depends on the involvement of multiple jurisdictions, levels of government, functional agencies, and/or emergency-responder disciplines. These instances necessitate effective and efficient coordination across this broad spectrum of organizations and activities. By using NIMS, communities are part of a comprehensive national approach that improves the effectiveness of emergency management and response personnel across the full spectrum of potential threats and hazards (including natural hazards, terrorist activities, and other human-caused disasters) regardless of size or complexity.

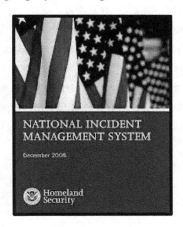

Incident Command System

The Incident Command System (ICS) is a management system designed to enable effective and efficient domestic incident management by integrating a combination of facilities, equipment, personnel, procedures, and communications operating within a common organizational structure. ICS is normally structured to facilitate activities in five major functional areas: command, operations, planning, logistics, Intelligence & Investigations, finance and administration. It is a fundamental form of management, with the purpose of enabling incident managers to identify the key concerns associated with the incident—often under urgent conditions—without sacrificing attention to any component of the command system.

The **Incident Commander is solely responsible for all management activities of an incident**. The decision-making process ends with the Incident Manager position. It is a daunting responsibility for anyone. The incident Command System enables integrated communication and planning by establishing a manageable span of control. ICS divides an emergency response into five manageable functions essential for emergency response operations: Command, Operations, Planning, Logistics, and Finance and Administration.

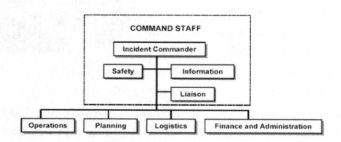

The IC is faced with many responsibilities when he/she arrives on scene. Unless specifically assigned to another member of the Command or General Staffs, these responsibilities remain with the IC. Some of the more complex responsibilities include:

> - Establish immediate priorities especially the safety of responders, other emergency workers, bystanders, and people involved in the incident.
> - Stabilize the incident by ensuring life safety and managing resources efficiently and cost effectively.
> - Determine incident objectives and strategy to achieve the objectives.
> - Establish and monitor incident organization.
> - Approve the implementation of the written or oral Incident Action Plan.
> - Ensure adequate health and safety measures are in place.

Command Staff

The Command Staff is responsible for public affairs, health and safety, and liaison activities within the incident command structure. The IC remains responsible for these activities or may assign individuals to carry out these responsibilities and report directly to the IC.

The **Information Officer's** role is to develop and release information about the incident to the news media, incident personnel, and other appropriate agencies and organizations.

The **Liaison Officer's** role is to serve as the point of contact for assisting and coordinating activities between the IC/UC and various agencies and groups. This may include Congressional personnel, local government officials, and criminal investigating organizations and investigators arriving on the scene.

The **Safety Officer's** role is to develop and recommend measures to the IC/UC for assuring personnel health and safety and to assess and/or anticipate hazardous and unsafe situations. The Safety Officer also develops the Site Safety Plan, reviews the Incident Action Plan for safety implications, and provides timely, complete, specific, and accurate assessment of hazards and required controls.

General Staff

The **General Staff** includes Operations, Planning, Logistics, and Finance/Administrative responsibilities. These responsibilities remain with the IC until they are assigned to another individual. When the Operations, Planning, Logistics or Finance / Administrative responsibilities are established as separate functions under the IC, they are managed by a section chief and can be supported by other functional units.

- The **Operations** Staff is responsible for all operations directly applicable to the primary mission of the response.
- The **Planning** Staff is responsible for collecting, evaluating, and disseminating the tactical information related to the incident, and for preparing and documenting Incident Action Plans (IAP's).
- The **Logistics** Staff is responsible for providing facilities, services, and materials for the incident response.
- The **Finance and Administrative** Staff is responsible for all financial, administrative, and cost analysis aspects of the incident.

The following is a list of Command Staff and General Staff responsibilities that either the IC or UC of any response should perform or assign to appropriate members of the Command or General Staffs:

- Provide response direction;
- Coordinate effective communication;
- Coordinate resources;
- Establish incident priorities;
- Develop mutually agreed-upon incident objectives and approve response strategies;
- Assign objectives to the response structure;
- Review and approve IAP's;
- Ensure integration of response organizations into the ICS
- Establish protocols;
- Ensure worker and public health and safety; and
- Inform the media.

In Usage

The Incident Command System (ICS) is modular and flexible. No emergency is the same, and as such, no response to all emergencies can be the same. ICS allows for few people in the case of a wildfire burning amongst two counties requiring them to work in conjunction with each other; or ICS can be expanded to respond to an incident a large as Hurricane Katrina require 1000's more responders.

Not all functions and capabilities of ICS, such as "finance", may be required in other areas. Only the parts required, need to be utilized.

Dangerous Texas Wildlife

The State Of Texas has any number of wildlife that might pose a threat to Texas State Guardsmen when responding to an accident, natural disaster, or other incident. Amongst those threats would be anything from insects, canine's, and reptiles, up to big cats, and bears.

Some of the most common threats are: Bees, Wasps, Fire Ants, Scorpions, Spiders, Mountain Lions, and Snakes.

Bees

Texas has several types of bees including Honey Bees and Bumble Bees. Most bees establish hives in Spring and Fall. Contrary to common belief, Honey Bees are the only bees with a barbed stinger that can only sting one time. Honey bees get to about 1/2 inch in size, while Bumble Bees are thicker around their bodies and grow to about 3/4th an inch. Bees vary in color from yellow and light brown-to-black. Honey bees tend to occupy elevated hives, while bumble bees nest in, or close to, the ground.

Africanized Killer Bees are a type of hybrid Honey Bee that was being studied in an attempt to increase honey yields. During the Brazilian study, several Queen bees were accidentally/mistakenly released into South America. The queens attacked and replaced the queens of local Honey Bee species and their aggressive "Killer" offspring are the result.

They have been dubbed "Killer Bees" because they have evolved to be hyper-defensive of their hive and their queen. They are more aggressive than the bee colonies common within the Americas prior to their release. Since their accidental release, they began migration from South America, through Central America, and are currently in North America. They are considered an Invasive Species.

How to escape Bees

RUN! Run away from the hive or swarm. Get as far away from them, as fast as you can. A quarter of a mile may be required. If the bees are Africanized Killer bees, they may chase you for up to a half-mile. You don't have to run fast, but you have to run. Run and then get medical assistance. Bee venom is poisonous and too much will likely lead to Anaphylactic Shock. If you do not run… YOU WILL DIE.

What to Do If Stung By A Bee

1. Write down the time of the sting
2. Remove the stinger and the attached poison sac
   a. By scraping it from the skin with a dull edge (e.g., the edge of a credit card.)
   b. Do not pinch the stinger to remove it.

Wasps

Texas has several species of "wasps", generically labeled as, Hornets. Wasp stingers are not barbed, which allows for multiple stings. Any pain felt pain is intense, but brief. The area around a sting, may see some localized swelling, however, any symptoms should subside within a few brief hours.

The most common type of wasp, are Yellow Jackets. They are 1/2 inch long. They are generally black with yellow markings around their head's and bodies. They are typically calm, and mind their own business; however, they can become aggressive when they are searching for food.

Mud Daubers are another common wasp, they grow up to 3/4 to one inch long. They are typically black, blueish-black, or black and yellow. These are the wasps that build mud based hanging caves on the side of shaded structures. Although, they can sting, they usually are attempting to display dominance and will fake attacks.

Fire Ants

Fire Ants are an aggressive type of ant that comes in four species within Texas. Just like human Texans are when defending their persons and property, Fire Ants are quick to respond when their colony is attacked. Just as other ants, they can either sting you repeatedly, or bite you repeatedly. When they sting, some humans may discover they are sensitive to the venom and might require medical attention. Occasionally, Fire Ants kill humans and should be treated as exceptionally dangerous.

Fire Ants can grow up to ¼ inch long, and range in color from dark brown to a light reddish-brown. Their colonies tend to be large, buried, and they are to be avoided when possible.

Scorpions

There are more than 18 species of scorpions in Texas. Most of the Texas scorpion species reside within the Big Bend region (West Texas). Scorpion stings are not generally considered to be life-threatening (for humans), but the stings may cause some excruciatingly sharp pain, which can produce some local reactions. It is important to note that Arizona and New Mexico do have scorpion species that are deadly to humans, and just because humans recognize the State borders, does not mean scorpions do. A scorpion's venom is neurotoxic; therefore, it is incumbent that we observe anyone who gets stung. Texas' indigenous scorpions tend to range from 2 to 4 inches in length. The color of the most common scorpions within Texas vary from dark brown to near translucent.

NOTE: Always be cautions. Regardless of what you may have heard. Small, young scorpions can inject the same amount of venom as adult scorpions. It's best to leave them alone.

Spiders

Spiders serve a very beneficial purpose in nature, often feeding on nuisance critters such as mosquitoes, gnats, flies, crickets. All spiders have venom; that is how they kill their prey. However, most bites are not usually not medically significant, with the exception of, bites from widow spiders and recluse spiders. If you are bitten by a spider, you may experience a red, swollen, itchy area on your skin. In most cases, these go away without much care or attention. If you feel or see the spider biting you, wash the area with soap and water.

Tarantulas

Tarantulas are large hairy spiders. They are brown to black in color, and adults can grow to over three inches long. They may be seen in the evenings when they are hunting for food. Males can sometimes be seen in larger numbers during warmer months. If you find one crawling, get your camera and take a picture, but just leave it alone.

Tarantulas are not aggressive spiders and only bite when cornered or feel threatened. They do possess venom, but here is no evidence that any of their venoms are lethal (to humans). Bites MAY be painful and cause unpleasant symptoms, and resemble a bee sting, but you will survive. Tarantulas can also brush hairs off their abdomen into humans, which can be irritating to the skin or eyes.

Recluse Spiders

Recluse Spiders are a common spider within Texas. They are also called "Brown Recluse", "Fiddle-Back", "Violin Spiders", or as "Reapers". They are associated with fiddles or violins, because of the violin-shaped markings that are located on its back. This marking is shared amongst the thousands of spiders of the Recluse family. The body size is

1/4 to 3/4 inches long. When you add the leg span, you are looking at about an inch and a half in size. Recluse spiders live in dark, secluded, moist spots such as under fallen trees or under beds (such as those found in nearly every Texas home). These tendencies lend support to the name "Recluse".

Most Recluse bites are unremarkable; however, some bites will cause immediate severe pain. On the unfortunate and scary side, Recluse venom is extremely toxic to humans and can cause skin and muscle to die. Bites can erupt into scary, disturbing looking, open, ulcerated, necrotic lesions, where the skin dies from the venom. Internet imagery of such lesions is usually horrific.

Widow Spiders

"Widow" Spiders refers to a class of spiders. There are about 32 species in the class and Texas has several. The most well-known and feared is the Southern Black Widow. The Black Widow has become synonymous with venomous spiders in the United States, although it is not as dangerous as its name alludes. 'Widows keep to themselves and live in outdoor areas that are fairly isolated where they can hunt in peace.

Males may get to be .75 inches. The Widow to be cautious of is the female. They can become 1.5 inches long and wear the familiar red marking on the underside of their bodies/abdomen that appears to be a red (or white, orange, pink, yellow, or brown) hourglass. Females generally bite when threatened or when attempting to protect their offspring. Widow venom can cause intense pain for 1 - 3 hours and may lead to medical issues in some humans if untreated, but usually do not end in hospitalization or death.

The "Widow" in their name refers to the act in which the females would mate with the males... and then eat them. This sexual-cannibalism has been observed in lab settings, however, does not generally occur when food is readily available.

> **What To Do If Stung or Bitten by Insects/Spiders**
>
> 1) Write down the time of the Sting or Bite.
> 2) Remove stinger if applicable
> 3) Wash with soap and water
> 4) Determine (ask) the victim if they are allergic to any known insect stings or bites.
> 5) Observe the individual bitten
> 6) If patient develops breathing problems, wheezing or swelling around the lips or tongue,

Mountain Lions

Texas has a sizable Mountain Lion population. They are generally elusive and solitary, and do not normally attack humans, however, if sick or hungry, it is possible. There have been several attacks on humans within Texas in the past few years, but it is extremely rare.

Mountain lions have been spotted in more counties within TX and may be expanding their range as humans spread into their habitat. It may also be that due to information and knowledge, humans are informing authorities when they see one, and more such sightings are being reported.

Mountain lions are generally light brownish in color but may appear to be extremely dark/black depending on lighting and time of day. They can grow to be between 100 – 170 pounds. American Mountain Lions may be called names such as Cougars, Panthers, or even Puma.

Snakes

Snakes generally bite humans when they are surprised, or threatened. Texas has four venomous snakes types. These include (1) Rattlesnakes, (2) Copperheads, (3) Water Moccasins, and (4) Coral snakes.

Rattlesnakes

There are more than a dozen rattlesnakes species in Texas. They include the Timber Rattler, Mojave, and the Western Diamond Back.  Rattlesnakes are pit vipers. The pits on their heads detect heat and when the snake bites, it shoots venom through its fangs and into the victim. Pit vipers generally have triangular-shaped heads. As thusly named, they have a rattles on their tails.

Rattlesnakes generally give you that familiar rattle warning when a human gets too close or they feel threatened, but; ALWAYS be cautious, because they have adapted to their predators such as feral hogs; and because of this, may strike without warning.

Copperheads

There are three different types of Copperheads found in Texas. The Broadband Copperhead, the Southern Copperhead, and the Trans-Pecos Copperhead. The Broadband, and Southern Copperheads live in much of the State, however, the Trans-Pecos Copperhead is limited to the Far West Texas area (Big Bend). Copperheads are also pit vipers. They have the pits on their heads and they are, called Copperheads due to their appearance. They are; copper colored. They have dark brown hour glass patterns on their bodies to distinguish them from other snakes.

Cottonmouth Water Moccasin

Generally referred to only as "Cottonmouth", the Cottonmouth Water Moccasin is North Americas only venomous water snake. They are olive, brown to black and have a lighter colored belly. Cottonmouths are aggressive, dangerous predators (that can swim). They do not run from dangers, but instead may approach or attack those who it perceives as threats.

It is normal for a Cottonmouth to have its mouth open. When open, the white insides of his mouth are exposed, leading to its name, Cottonmouth. RUN from them, they're NOT afraid of you.

Coral Snakes

The fourth snake is a coral snake which is not a viper. Its head is basically the same size as the rest of the body, it has round eyes, and 1/8-inch-long fixed rear fangs. The coral snake found in Texas is the only black, red, and yellow cross-banded snake with the red and yellow bands touching. "Red against yellow kills a fellow, red against black, poison lack." It can be confused with the king, milk, or scarlet snakes, which have bands of similar color. The snake's small fangs

do not penetrate well so many bites do not inject venom. Coral Snakes are typically very small; growing to about 26 inches."

> Dealing with snakes and snake bites:
>
> Avoid habitat areas IF POSSIBLE and KNOWN
>
> 1) Remain Calm
> 2) Elevate the bitten area level to heart
> 3) Write down the time of the bite and,
> 4) remove jewelry or other items (Specifically Rings)
>   a. Write a description of the snake
> 5) Rinse and Wash the bitten area
> 6) Cover with a Cloth
> 7) What NOT to do
>   a. Cut the wound and try to extract the venom.
>   b. Attempt to suck out the venom
>   c. Do not use ice over the bite
>   d. Do not Tourniquet.

Anti-venom treatment is available for the majority of Texas snakes in many of our hospitals. Observe TXSG Members who get bit and get them to appropriate medical attention as needed.

> For assistance regarding Snake Bites, Bees and Wasps, Scorpions, Spiders, or other venomous lifeforms, call Poison Control at:
>
> **1-800-222-1222**
>
> Or visit
>
> **www.PoisonControl.org**

Be Careful

Texas is a rugged place, and the animals and critters must be rugged to survive. When operating in much of remote Texas, TXSG members, should NEVER be surprised by what they may find out there. Whether it is exotic African animals such as Nilgai, Zebra, or Oryx; or Panthers or Ocelot. It is important that all TXSG members pay attention to our surroundings and keep an eye on our fellow TXSG personnel.

Remember that much of the property you may find yourself on may be private property. Be respectful to all Texas lands, of Ranchers, or other property owners encountered.

NOTES:

Communications

The Land Mobile Radio

Land Mobile Radios (LMRs) are hand held two-way radios that may consist of a combination of larger base station transmitters, and one or more portable/mobile radio units. Generally, they are referred to as "hand-held" radios This radio system provides communications when telephones or other communication systems can't satisfy mission essential requirements. **All LMR systems use line-of-sight waves to make communication possible.**

"Line-of-sight" characteristics means you may or may not receive all radio transmissions. This is due in part to your location in relation to the transmitting LMR antenna. To increase radio reception and transmission minimize any potential interference between your location and the LMR antenna. Potential interference can include buildings, dense forestry, hardened shelters, or close proximity to other LMR stations.

Radio usage varies throughout the many TXSG units, however, numerous types of hand-held radios are in common usage. The radios all consist of similar components such as; the Body, Antennae, transmit button, Frequency and Channel knobs.

Radios must be programmed to work on a specific channel. This is usually done with a laptop computer; however, more specific information is required regarding which frequency TXSG will be allowed to use. This information is determined by location, radio, and any military units assigned to the area. Communications personnel will determine this and program the radios prior to their use for any given operation. Some common terms regarding handheld radios or radio networks would include:

Base Station: Consist of a larger, non-mobile radio transmitter and receiver antenna, microphone, and interconnecting hardware.

Cellular Phone: A battery powered portable telephone that works over a radio-frequency network. Modern cell phones, not only transmit voice communications but also text messages.

Mobile Radio: Generally, mobile refers to a radio station located in a vehicle. This unit operates off the power provided by the vehicle or trailer generator. Because of this power generation, they can usually be more powerful than handheld radios

Portable Radio: A battery powered "handheld" two-way radio. This is what TXSG personnel are most likely to use (save, cell phones)

Repeater: Increases the range of a radio network. The repeater receives a radio signal, amplifies it, and retransmits it simultaneously. This allows communication between distant locations if a repeater is between two distant radios.

Radio Messages

Radio Messages are composed of 3 requirements.

1. *'Who From*
2. *'Who To*
3. *'Concise Message*

As an example of a complete and specific message. Look below as one post attempts to ask another post a question, and as the second post responds

EXAMPLE:

> *"Sierra 1 to Bravo 3 - Does your post need any assistance?"*

RESPONSE:

> *"Bravo 3 to Sierra 1 - Negative, We do not require assistance."*

Both posts identified themselves, identified whom they were responding to. And they answered or asked the appropriate question. Using a radio can cause a bit of anxiety when not familiar or experienced however, there are some ways to alleviate any concerns. Some steps might include:

- ✓ Preplan your message before transmitting
- ✓ Make only authorized transmissions
- ✓ Listen before transmitting
- ✓ Transmit clearly and accurately
- ✓ Use the phonetic alphabet
- ✓ Maintain transmission security

Treat radio as though the FCC or a enemy is listening. If you are contemplating sending information that you are not certain would be good if in the wrong hands, do NOT transmit it. Always err on the side of caution. Some items that we should ALWAYS avoid include:

> **DO NOT EVER:**
>
> 1) Hold personal or unofficial conversations
>
> 2) Transmit personal information (names, SSN, etc.)
>
> 3) Use unauthorized pro-words (I.e. Repeat)
>
> 4) Use profanity
>
> 5) Mention who is in Command
>
> 6) Lose possession of your radio

Personally Identifiable Information (PII)

NEVER Transmit P.I.I Over Radio!

Personally Identifiable Information (PII) is any information about an individual that identifies, links, relates, or is unique to him or her. This also includes information which can be used to distinguish or trace an individual's identity and any other personal information which is linked or linkable to a specific individual.

Establish good PII handling behaviors. Some behaviors are to:

> - NEVER leave PII, or any Computers/Drives containing PII unattended.
> - Do not collect PII when it can be avoided
> - Destroy PII when no longer required
> - Label all PII. In the subject line of email, use the label "FOUO". In the body of the email, write "FOR OFFICIAL USE ONLY"

It is incumbent on ALL TXSG members to protect the PII, and privacy of EVERY OTHER TXSG member. All information that can be used to identify a person can be considered PII. Some common examples of PII would include:

- First, Middle, and/or Last
- Age / Date and place of birth
- Social Security Number
- Driver's license number
- Mother's maiden name
- Demographic information
- Financial account or credit card numbers
- Medical information

Call Signs

Call Signs are pre-assigned names designated to individuals, posts, or patrols. They are codenames used to add an additional measure of safety and security. They help ensure that only those who are authorized to use the radio have an advantage of understanding whom is being communicated to.

Instead of calling an individual by name and rank, the Call Sign clarifies who is communicating. Call Signs are also used to denote posts or static patrols. This ensures that anyone monitoring your radio communications. They may hear the communication, but may not know who is involved.

EXAMPLE: Instead of referring for *"Colonel Sanders"* on the radio; refer to, *"Falcon 1"* (or any other pre-defined name).

EXAMPLE: Instead of calling to *"the post on the main gate"*, over the radio; *"Golf 1"* (or Gate 1) is used.

Radio Security

Even when utilizing "Secure" radios, communications cannot be 100% safe from hacking or interception. So, for technical and logistical purposes, certain protocols have been put in place to ensure the security of all assets of the DoD and its forces. Among radio security protocols, are Duress Words, and Procedure-Words.

Duress Words

A word or phrase that can be easily used in a conversation, to alert personnel the user is acting against their own will. When properly used, the code should alert security, or law enforcement know that a possible duress situation exists and give the user a reasonable level of personal safety.

1. The duress code must be protected by the following measures:
   - Revealing it only to those who need to know it.
   - Changing it every six months or when compromise is suspected.

Examples of Duress words may include: Angel, Brunch, Cardinal, Droopy, Entertain, Fashion, Gentile, Hotplate, etc.

The key is that they must be rare (in a security setting) but common enough to be used in language.

Pro-words

To keep radio transmissions as short, concise, and as clear as possible, radio operators use procedure words (PROWORDs) to take the place of long sentences. Some of the more commonly used pro-words and their explanations would include:

PROWORD	EXPLANATION
AFFIRMATIVE	Yes --- I do --- we do,
ALL AFTER	I refer to all of the message that follows...
ALL BEFORE	I refer to all of the message that proceeds...
BREAK	I now separate the text from other parts of the message.
COPY	Understood
CORRECTION	There is an error in this transmission. Transmission continues with the last word correctly transmitted.
I SAY AGAIN	If the information is confusing and you need to say that information again.
I SPELL	I will spell the next word phonetically.
MORE TO FOLLOW	Transmitting station has additional traffic for the receiving station.
NEGATIVE	No --- I do not --- we do not
OUT	This is the end of my transmission to you and no answer is required or expected.
OVER	This is the end of my transmission to you and a Response is necessary. Go ahead transmit.
ROGER	I have received your last transmission satisfactorily.
SAY AGAIN	Repeat all your last transmission followed by identification data. [DO NOT USE "Repeat" as repeat has its own distinct meaning"]
STAND BY	Wait for a moment, or Pay Attention to what follows. Do not attempt to transmit
WILCO	"<u>WIL</u>l <u>CO</u>mply" -- I have received your transmission, understand it and will comply.

The Phonetic Alphabet

On radio or phone communications, there may be a need to spell out a word in order to ensure a message is understood when sent between individuals or posts. The phonetic alphabet is used to clarify and limit the chances of miscommunication.

A	ALPHA	(AL FAH)
B	BRAVO	(BRAH VOH)
C	CHARLIE	(CHAR LEE)
D	DELTA	(DELL TAH)
E	ECHO	(ECK OH)
F	FOXTROT	(FOKS TROT)
G	GOLF	(GOLF)
H	HOTEL	(HOH TELL)
I	INDIA	(IN DEE AH)
J	JULIETT	(JEW LEE ETT)
K	KILO	(KEY LOH)
L	LIMA	(LEE MAH)
M	MIKE	(MIKE)
N	NOVEMBER	(NO VEM BER)
O	OSCAR	(OSS CAH)
P	PAPA	(PAH PAH)
Q	QUEBEC	(KEH BECK)
R	ROMEO	(ROW ME OH)
S	SIERRA	(SEE AIR RAH)
T	TANGO	(TANG GO)
U	UNIFORM	(YOU NEE FORM)
V	VICTOR	(VIK TAH)
W	WHISKEY	(WISS KEY)
X	XRAY	(ECKS RAY)
Y	YANKEE	(YANG KEY)
Z	ZULU	(ZOO LOO)
1	ONE	(WUN)
2	TWO	(TOO)

3	THREE	(TREE)
4	FOUR	(FOW ER)
5	FIVE	(FIFE)
6	SIX	(SIX)
7	SEVEN	(SEV EN)
8	EIGHT	(AIT)
9	NINE	(NIN ER)
0	ZERO	(ZE RO)

EXAMPLE: *"Our current location is on Lassent St."*

This would no doubt be confusing on radio due to being an uncommon word that includes, double S', an "e" that may be confused with an "I", and a "t" at the end, that may not be clear over radio. It may be beneficial to spell the street name out over radio. *You instead might say:*

"Our current location is on, I spell, (pause) LIMA – ALPHA – SIERRA – SIERRA – ECHO – NOVEMBER–TANGO, (pause) street", Copy?

If the message was received and understood, the post you are communicating with will/may reply with:

"Copy!"

Radio Etiquette

When sharing a network with others, we must ensure that we treat the network as a valuable resource that we share. We must be cognizant and courteous to our TXSG members on the network.

➢	Always wait until an on-going interaction is complete. Even if that requires that you wait momentarily, allow those communicating time to address their issues
➢	Slow down and allow those on the radio time to process what you are saying.
➢	Avoid excessively long transmissions in favor of direct, but short, messages. Instead of speaking a paragraph. Speak 4 short sentences with pauses in between.
➢	Release the radio's transmit button after you speak.
➢	NEVER Interrupt the transmissions of others unless it is an emergency. --- To intentionally interrupt for an emergency, state "Break, Break, Break". And state your emergency.
➢	NEVER use the word "Repeat". "Repeat" means to DO the last action that was completed. Example: If an artillery unit has fired off rounds in a location. Ordering them to "Repeat" would be telling them to fire again. Avoid confusion, use the pro-word, "I Say Again", instead of "Repeat."

Communications Status Check (Why and How)

Do NOT forget Conduct Communications status checks!

Communications Status Checks are completed to ensure that all posts and patrols are still alert, attentive, and unharmed. Additionally, a 'Comm Status Check, ensures that radios are still operating and that batteries have not died. It is standard to conduct radio status checks randomly, not to exceed 90 minutes to ensure the safety, and security of all posts and patrols. A standard 'Comm Status Check might sound like this example:

> "Charlie 1 (or Command Post call sign) to all posts and patrols, this office will be conducting a security status check… beginning with Post #1"
>
> [pause]
>
> "Post #1 -- What is your status?"
>
> (Post #1 replies) -- "Post #1 is All Secure."
>
> [pause]
>
> "Post #2, What is your status?"
>
> (Post #2 replies) -- "Post #2 is All Secure."
>
> [pause]
>
> "Post #3, What is your status?"
>
> (Post #3 replies) -- "Post #3 is All Secure."
>
> [pause]
>
> After all posts have responded, [Command Post call sign] will acknowledge by stating:
>
> "Charlie 1 (or Command Post Call sign) to all posts and patrols: All posts are secure at this time."

    If a Communications Status Check is completed and posts could not be contacted? The priority becomes to clear the network and send someone cautiously to them to ensure that they are safe and accounted for.

TICP

Texas Interoperability Communications Protocol (TICP) are communications trailers that are part of **Task Force Signal**. They are operated by the Texas Army, Air National Guard, as well as the Texas State Guard. They are deployed to ensure that in cases of emergency. Communication can be made to remote parts of the state when other communications are non-available. The individual TICP units can use radio, or connect to Satellites for communication. They can also provide Internet service to remotely detailed units. TICP's serve important functions including:

- Communicate with other TICP units
- Operate as a remote communications hub
- Transmit messages through Satellites
- Transmit data over radio
- Provide Internet service via WiFi Hotspots
- Download Video from aircraft, such as Homeland Security or Department Of Defense Drones/UAVs

Pulling A TICP

Pulling a TICP can be daunting, and dangerous. It is an extremely heavy trailer with a lot of weight. Every step must be taken to successfully and safely transport the unit from its origin to its operating destination. Skill and attention must thoroughly be paid to ensure that the trailer is hooked up, and towed correctly.

This is especially important considering that it will be towed on roads where the lives of other Texans will be at risk.

- Ensure Stabilizer bars are attached
- Inspect your equipment before you use it
- Write down any issues with the unit
- Ensure the trailer is on, AND secure on the hitch ball
- Ensure the safety chains are connected
- Double check all tires for pressure (tow vehicle and trailer)
- Do load checks to ensure gear is stowed/secured
- Ensure the brakes are working
- Ensure the trailer is setup and maintained
- NEVER exceed the speed limit of the equipment
- Maintain situational awareness of the traffic around you
- Use a spotter when backing the unit

Other than those basic notes, pay attention to what you've learned in Training. Be cognizant the weight of the trailer, the length, the fuel types required. Most importantly, ensure you clear the height of the boom/mast when deploying. A TICP costs a lot of money, so treat it as though it is a valuable state asset, because it is.

Communications Security (COMSEC)

Due to the nature of the Texas State Guard, we may during times of turmoil be required to utilize hand-held radios. Experience shows us that during times of natural disaster, Communications systems are usually non-functional. As an example, during a Hurricane, Cellular towers may be destroyed, damaged, or may not have power to allow them to function. When cellular networks are no longer available, hand-held radios become our primary means of communication.

We must use whatever means available that allows us to maintain contact with each other and complete the task at hand. It is important that we are aware of our usage.

Radios and cellular phones are a **non-secure** means of communications.

All TXSG telecommunications are subject to monitoring. Using any government telecommunication system or device constitutes subject to monitoring by the Federal Communications Commission.

Essential Elements of Friendly Information (EEFI) are small bits of information gathered from different sources that are used to build other information that may be used against the United States or its allies.

Guard Duty

"Guard Duty", "Posting", and/or "Standing Watch" is a traditional function of military operations. As such, many of the duties the TXSG conducts may include being posted at locations such as gates, doors, command posts, or shelter facilities. Along with "soldiering," guard duty is one of the oldest functions of military forces within the United States.

General Orders

Each branch of the US military has included functions of Standing Guard/Watch into its General Orders. **General Orders are basic orders that personnel use as the baseline set of instructions required to stand on guard duty.**

All US Military General orders for posts and sentries are similar and all have the EXACT same Origins; the Continental Army of George Washington. The US Navy General Orders, are based upon the US Army General Orders. The US Marine Corps General Orders are based upon the US Navy AND Army General Orders, and the US Air Force Security Forces General Orders are based upon the General Orders of the US Army and Marine Corps.

The Air Force Security Forces are the Military Police (formerly "Air Police," and "Security Police") of the Air Force and are responsible for, not only Military Policing, but also aircraft security, Airbase Defense, K-9, nuclear security, Force Protection, and Anti-Terrorism. They are the force that are armed on Air Force Bases at any given moment, Their THREE General Orders are succinct, compact, and are a basic model that may be used by TXSG members standing Guard/Watch while conducting the business of the TXSG. Those orders are as follows:

General Order #1

"I will take charge of my post and protect personnel and property for which I am responsible until properly relieved."

General Order #2

"I will report all violation of orders I am instructed to enforce and will call my superior in any case not covered by instructions."

General Order #3

"I will sound the alarm in case of disorder or emergency."

Whichever component you are a part of, it is important to know your posts Primary Duties, and Post Limits.

PRIMARY DUTIES: Know what the Primary duties of your post is. If there is a post… it must have a function. If your post does not have a Primary duty, how do you know if you are being effective on that post? Some primary duties would include; controlling entry to a shelter, directing traffic in a particular direction, or verifying identification of people entering a facility.

POST LIMITS: Know what your post limits are. It is incumbent for security and safety that everyone, that the person posted, is aware of their post limits. If you are supposed to be controlling access to a gate, and you leave the gate and people are not aware of where you are, that becomes a vulnerability and may put security at risk. Or if you leave the post, your unit may determine that you have become injured, or are in danger.

By following the General orders, It goes without saying, that you should **NEVER LEAVE YOUR POST** without being relieved, or otherwise without direct permission. If you do, not only is your post uncontrolled, but the people who believe you are supposed to be there, have lost track of you. This IS an emergency.

It is important to note that at the current time, there are no specific, official TXSG General Orders so it is incumbent on all members to pay attention to the orders of their specific units or components. It is worthy to note that; **YOU CANNOT GO WRONG IF YOU DO FOLLOW THE ABOVE GENERAL ORDERS.** In the end; the General Orders are common sense. They tell you to: (1) Pay attention to what's going on around your post, (2) Call your Supervisor if you have any issues, and (3) Let someone know immediately when/if there is a problem.

Circulation Control and the Entry Authority List (EAL)

Circulation Control: is **the positive control of entry, exit and internal movement of personnel, vehicles and material within an area.** Controlling how personnel, customers, and clients move within an area may help ensure efficient flow of operations, avoid confusion of those we are trying to assist, and generally promote a more orderly TXSG response in an emergency situation.

Utilize efficient circulation control measures when moving personnel through processing lines, or anywhere order is required to assist large numbers of people, or to assist personnel through a chaotic process. Some examples of good circulation control measures are:

- ✓ Signage or posted directed
- ✓ Separate entry and exit points (doors)
- ✓ Logical order ("table 1", "table 2", ect...)

Entry Control is utilized for many areas that the TXSG may be required to post upon. In areas where access is to be controlled such as a headquarters facility, command post, emergency operations center (EOC), a shelter, or even a medical facility where TX Medical Brigade personnel are serving a group of individuals, a method of controlling access may be required. The most efficient means is by using an Entry Authority List (EAL).

An EAL is:

A list usually containing any combination of an individual's name, rank, social security number, identification number, organization, of personnel designated as having authority to enter a specific area. EAL's are used as a supporting technique for limiting access into certain areas.

When establishing any posts, always consider circulation control. Recognize that once a post is established of entry and exit when possible. It is a constant goal for personnel controlling a facility to know who is inside the facility at any given time.

NOTES:

Common Hand and Arm Signals

Hand and Arm signals are a necessary function of military operations. It is important to recognize a few common hand and arm signals because they may be utilized by National Guard, Air National Guard, and DoD personnel during emergency responses.

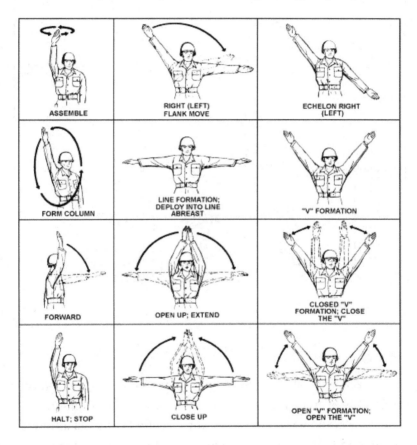

Because these hand and arm signals have been utilized by US Forces for so long, they are also adopted to Emergency Responders, Police Agencies, as well as Air and Boat Crews.

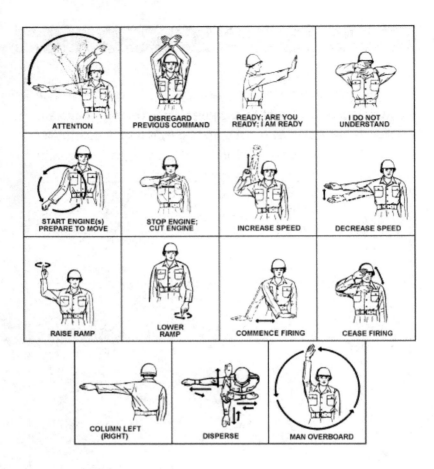

Directing Automotive Traffic

Hand signals change when it comes to directing automotive traffic. The average driver may not be aware of the common military or emergency hand signs, they will understand a intuitive "come to me" arm signal, or a hand up, palm facing their vehicle stop signal. There are no right or wrong signals, so long as you use the same signals for all drivers; AND the drivers understand what the signals mean.

Directing traffic can be dangerous. Any time a human places himself in vehicular traffic, there are risks to human life. It is incumbent that if, in the case of emergency, TXSG members must direct vehicle traffic, every possible safety measure be taken to ensure that we do not become victims of traffic. What can we do to minimize the danger:

- CONTROL THE TRAFFIC. Use positive movements to direct traffic. When you want a vehicle to stop, focus on the driver, until he has your attention.
- Make eye contact with drivers when you're giving them directions. This helps you know that they see you.
- Stand in a visible location. Position yourself so that moving traffic must deviate its logical path if it is to make contact with you.
- Use High-Visibility tools. Hi-Vis Orange, or Hi-Vis green traffic vests and flashlights in both day or night.
- Utilize a partner to observe any dangerous situations that may be taking place, and serve as an additional set of eyes.
- Be confident and engaging. Drivers will respect your presence better if they feel you know what you're doing.
- Direct traffic until you are no longer needed! This may require you to clear (exit) the intersection and observe how traffic flows without your presence. Drivers will generally establish a right-of-way system on their own, or resort to logical, flow plan.

In the end, it is common sense that will keep traffic moving, and will keep everyone safe. All traffic control stems from the idea that the individual directing traffic should **be in a position to see traffic AND to be seen by the traffic being directed.**

Customs and Courtesies

Whether we are Enlisted, Warrant Officer, or Officers, we are all TXSG members who must protect each other. We are all volunteers, and we are all Texans. It is incumbent on all of us to be courteous to each other and to ensure we utilize mutual respect. We all are expected to treat each other in a manner that befits a professional military organization.

Military customs are established practices used within the military community. Courtesies are those expectations of being courteous that military personnel utilize when addressing each other. Some common Customs and Courtesies include:

- Standing-up when Sr. Enlisted and Officers enter the room.
- When addressing an individual senior to yourself, turn your body to them and stand at attention (depending on the situation) until acknowledge to do otherwise
- If you don't know the answer to a direct question, simply state, "I don't know, sir (or ma'am), but I'll find out." -- ...And then follow-up, and find out!

Chain of Command

Following your Chain of Command, is essential to the good order and discipline of the TXSG. The Chain of Command is to be used as a tool to ensure the most efficient and effective means of communication between the lowest, and the highest ranks within our organization.

If you bring an issue to your Chain of Command, and it is not resolved, it is acceptable to cautiously, sparingly, and respectfully, approach the individual next-higher in the chain of command if the issue is important.

The Chain of Command is NOT meant to reduce the effectiveness of a unit. It is meant to unify command and ensure our organization runs as efficiently and effectively as possible. There are some basic rules-of-thumb, and courtesies we utilize to ensure effective operation of our organization.

- Never act insubordinate or disrespectful toward a superior ranked TXSG member.

- Avoid coarse and insolent language to any member of the TXSG.

- Always report for duty at the time prescribed. A good rule of thumb is; "to arrive 15 minutes earlier than expected"

- Always appear clean, dry, and tidy, when in public.

- NEVER be overbearing, oppressive, or tyrannical in the discharge of TXSG duties.

- NEVER make false official statements.

If we work together closely, the TXSG can improve our functionality and ensure the safety of ourselves while conducting activities for our State.

The Military Salute

The military salute is a sign of respect. The salute goes back for thousands of years. Although there are multiple theories regarding how the military salute came about, one of the more enduring theories is based upon the Knighthood. Knights were covered in armor from head to toe, and the theory states that honorable knights lifted their visors to show their eyes and faces so other knights they encountered knew whom they were. This visor salute also showed that the Knight was not in a hostile posture since one would not engage an enemy with his visor up.

We Salute by sharply raising our straight forearm and the fingers of our right hand to the brim of our headgear, or eyebrow when we are not wearing cover (cap/hat/helmet).

A salute is rendered:

- ☑ To Military Officers
- ☑ When the United States National Anthem, "To the Color," "Hail to the Chief," or foreign national anthems are played
- ☑ To uncased National flag, or the Texas flag
- ☑ On ceremonial occasions, such as changes of command or funerals
- ☑ At reveille and retreat ceremonies, during the raising or lowering of the flag
- ☑ When pledging allegiance to the U.S. flag outdoors
- ☑ To officers of friendly/Allied foreign nations.

Salutes are not required when:

- ☒ Indoors, unless reporting to an officer (receiving an award)
- ☒ When on duty as a guard
- ☒ Saluting is obviously inappropriate

Treat all Officers, regardless of their Branch of the Military, Components, Services, or even Allied Nations, as you treat TXSG Officers, and render a salute if you acknowledge that they are Officers. This will include whether they are US Army, Navy, California Military Reserve (a State Defense Force), or even Australian, Canadian or British Officers. Salutes are free, while disrespecting an allied military Officer may be long lasting. Although it is not "illegal" NOT to salute, disrespect to a Commissioned, or Warrant, Officer is illegal. "When in doubt, Render a salute."

Representing the Texas State Guard

Gifts, gratuities, fees, rewards, loans -- Members shall not, under any circumstance, solicit any gift, gratuity, loan, or fee where there is any direct or indirect connection between the solicitation and their TXSG membership.

Intoxicants on department premises -- Members shall not possess any intoxicants while conducting TXSG business.

Misrepresentation and falsification -- No member shall, in an official capacity, knowingly misrepresent any matter, sign any false official statement or report, commit perjury, or give false testimony before any court, grand jury, board, commission, or official hearing.

Consorting -- Members of the TXSG should avoid personal association with persons who have an open and notorious reputation in the community for criminal behavior.

Business cards -- Business cards that refer to the TXSG shall be used by members only in connection with official TXSG business and shall be approved by the member's Commander.

Offensive material -- Members on duty shall not reproduce, circulate, or post any material that may be considered offensive on the basis of religion, race, ethnic origin, or sex.

Offensive statements -- Members shall not tell jokes or make statements or suggestions that may be considered offensive, based upon religion, race, ethnic origin, sex, or disability.

False injury claims -- Members injured off duty shall not falsely claim a job-related injury. Members shall not knowingly corroborate a false injury claim.

Appropriate attire -- Members must wear prescribed uniform or appropriate attire, while on duty. Refer to the respective uniform regulation.

Be respectful -- TXSG members should always treat all persons civilly and respectfully at all times.

Report violations -- Always report, to the proper Chain of Command, any member or employee guilty of violating TXSG rules, regulations, or orders.

In the end, representing the TXSG is simple, and at the heart of why we CHOOSE to volunteer our time and energy to the State. Never Conduct yourself in a manner unbecoming to a Texas State Guardsmen representing the state of Texas and/or be detrimental to the service.

The Lone Star Flag

The Texas State Flag, named, the Lone Star Flag, is required by law and tradition to be handled respectfully. The flag was introduced in December of 1838 to the Congress of the Republic of Texas. It was adopted in January of 1839. Texas became the 28th State within the United States on 29 December 1845.

Reverence is the word that is represented by the Lone Star Flag, both historically and in its usage. It is worthy to note, that because of the nickname of the "Lone Star Flag", that the nickname of the state became the, "Lone Star State".

The flag is NOT to be raised, upside-down. Doing so is a sign of distress and/or duress. An easy way to remember the proper orientation is by recognizing that:

"Blood Drips to The Ground"

The red stripe is below the white stripe. Another way to understand which way is up is by referencing the star. It is a 5-pointed star. The single point points to the sky.

When flags are hung vertically. The blue section is at the top and the single point is facing the left (which is the top of the flag). The Red Stripe is on the right.

Folding The State Flag

The state flag should be folded as follows:

1. Fold the flag in half lengthwise with the red stripe facing upward;
2. Fold the flag in half lengthwise once more, concealing the red stripe on the inside of the fold;
3. Position the flag with the white star facing downward and the blue stripe facing upward;
4. Fold the corner with the white stripe to the opposite side of the flag to form a triangle;
5. Continue folding the corners over in triangles until the resulting fold produces a blue triangle with a portion of the white star visible; and
6. Secure all edges into the folds.

A folded state flag should be presented or displayed with all folded edges secured and with the blue stripe and a portion of the white star visible. It should be stored or displayed in a manner that prevents tearing or soiling of the flag.

Hurricanes and Tornados

A large reason why the Texas State Guard Exists today is to respond to assist other Texans after they have been affected by Hurricanes or Tornados. It is essential that TXSG personnel pay attention to news and weather reports, and to the weather itself. Particularly be cautious of; dark, greenish gray skies, low-lying clouds, loud howling or roaring winds, and any clouds that appear to be rotating.

It is important for TXSG members to be alert to changing weather conditions and to remain on the lookout for approaching storms. Listen to NOAA Weather Radio or to commercial radio or television newscasts for the latest information. In any emergency, always listen to the instructions given by local emergency management officials.

Hurricanes

Hurricanes are severe storms that bring with them high winds. The hurricane winds travel in a spiral direction around an  "eye". The eye in the center may be calm. It may seem that since it is calm that the storm is over, however, wind will come, slightly more powerful, from the opposite direction as the eye of the storm passes. To qualify as a hurricane, the wind speeds must achieve 74 mph or greater.

Tropical "Waves," Tropical "Disturbances", or Tropical "Depressions" are storms that can develop into Tropical Storms or Hurricanes. Generally, these storms bring a maximum constant wind speed up to 38 mph. Tropical Storms can develop into Hurricanes when wind speeds achieve 39-74 mph. Tropical Storms warnings are generally issued within 24 hours of the storms expected arrival time.

Tropical "Waves", "Disturbances", "Depressions"	Winds up to 38 mph
Tropical "Storms"	Winds from 39-74 mph
Hurricane	Winds in excess of 74 mph

Tornados

A Tornado is a extremely violent twisting storm that reaches from cloud formations to the ground. They can form with

little time, and with little warning for those in the area. Tornados can push down trees, fling objects through walls and even demolish structures, such as houses. The most powerful tornadoes can bring winds of over 300 mph and can create swaths of damage more than two miles wide, for more than

35-50 miles long, destroying structures and lives in its path. Tornados are generally clear/transparent until dirt, debris, or moisture makes them visible. They average about 30 mph, but have been recorded at over 70 mph.

There are nearly 1000 (reported) tornadoes per year. Over 500 of these tornadoes happen in "Tornado Alley". Tornado Alley cuts a swath through Texas, Oklahoma, Kansas, Nebraska, South Dakota, North Dakota, Iowa, Missouri, Arkansas and Louisiana. Due to sheer size, Texas is the number one location within the United States (and the world) for incidents of Tornados with nearly 150 per year on average. Luckily, "most" tornadoes do not affect significant population centers, where large numbers of humans can be affected.

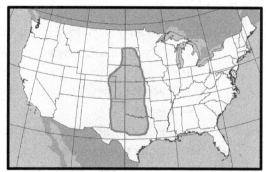

Tornado Watch	Tornadoes are possible. Remain alert for approaching storms. Watch the sky and stay tuned to NOAA Weather Radio, commercial radio or television for information.
Tornado Warning	A tornado has been sighted or indicated by weather radar. Take shelter immediately.

During a Hurricane or Tornado

Although the storms CAN generally come at any time, there MAY be weather related radio or TV reports. If you're paying attention, there should be days of heads up before hurricanes, and perhaps valuable minutes before tornadoes arrive. When possible, and time permitting, you should prepare by:

- Listen to the radio or TV for further information.
- Determine if you should stay at your home or you should evacuate
    - Evacuate if news outlets and local government suggest.
- Secure your home, close storm shutters, secure outdoor objects or bring them indoors.
    - Board up windows and secure your property.
- Turn off utilities if instructed to do so. Otherwise, turn the refrigerator thermostat to its coldest setting and keep its doors closed.
- Turn off propane tanks.
- Avoid using the phone, except for serious emergencies.
- Ensure a supply of water for sanitary purposes such as cleaning and flushing toilets. Fill the bathtub and other large containers with water.
- Close all interior doors—secure and brace external doors.
- Stay inside and away from windows, skylights and glass doors.
    - Keep curtains and blinds closed.
- Lie on the floor under a table or another sturdy object.
- Take refuge in a small interior room, closet, or hallway on the lowest level.

After a Hurricane or Tornado

You, as most other people will want to immediately get outside to see any damage that has occurred. There are some steps that we can take. Some of these items would be:

1. Do not go outside. Remain indoors until an official "all clear" is given.
    - It could merely be the eye of the storm.
2. Avoid lose or downed power lines
3. Watch for damaged or unstable trees or buildings
4. Use your phone for life-threatening emergencies ONLY
    - Leave it for those with actual emergency

Maintain A Storm Disaster Kit

In the event that a storm occurs in our areas, we must be prepared for natural disasters with an emergency kit. It is a basic collection of supplies you, or your family may need in the event of an emergency. The goal is to get you through the first 3-days of an event, when electricity, gas, water, and phone service may be unavailable. This kit should be assembled prior to an emergency because you may not have time to purchase or collect the supplies as the storm is approaching. Recommended items might include:

Drinking Water, one gallon of water per person per day for at least three days
A three-day supply of non-perishable (powdered, canned, packaged) food
Battery-powered or Hand cranked radio that can receive NOAA Weather transmissions.
Multiple Flashlights
Extra Batteries.

First aid kit
Wet wipes
Local maps
Cell phone with backup power source

If You Must Evacuate

If you have to evacuate because a storm is expected in your area. Take the warning and follow the recommendations of local government and the Weather Services. If there is time to prepare, use the valuable time wisely. It cannot hurt to add some items with you when you are evacuating by vehicle:

1. Road maps
2. Car repair items (tools, spare tire, Fix-A-Flat, oil
3. More food and water
4. Plastic plates, cups, utensils
5. Tent, blankets and pillows
6. Clothes and sturdy shoes
7. Rain gear and towels
8. Books, games, and toys

If time permits, remember to:

- ➢ Fill your gas tank, check your spare tire, if possible
- ➢ Take cash, checkbook and credit cards
- ➢ Call your family emergency contact
- ➢ Charge your mobile phone
- ➢ Have a map of your route

TXSG Email Usage

Composing emails will become a natural skill for all TXSG members since our organization is based upon internal communications. A majority of our communication is conducted via email for much of our activities outside of when we are physically present at Unit Training Activities (UTA), or Annual Training (AT).

Usage

When composing email, or any other TXSG product, always answer the questions of Who, What, Why, Where, and How. Ensure that you are sending a clearly understandable, and definable message.

- Be Consistent in your Quality (if packages look different and are composed differently every time, it makes it hard, and slower, for the user to efficiently review your work).
- For official letters, papers, promotion packages, or forms, follow examples. Refer to 600-10
- Use common fonts. Avoid "fancy" fonts, and stick with generally Arial, Calibri, or Times New Roman.

Signature Blocks

Use a Signature Block. Email is for to be treated as any other TXSG document and should identify it's sender. Your signature block should include at a MINIMUM your Name, Rank, and Unit: As an example:

MSG Sam Skinny
1st Regiment, TXSG

There are no specific rules, but to be professional. Keep any quotes short and tasteful if you choose to use them.

Legalities of TXSG Email

Using your TXSG email account IS using a State of Texas communications system. As such, all emails sent through the system are "Discoverable" in a court. Anything you write, transmit, and receive via TXSG email becomes official Texas State property, and thusly, becomes an Official Record. Only Use Texas State Guard email... for Official Use ONLY

Be Respectful. Ensure that you treat email communications as professionally. Be succinct, clear, and proofread, and spellcheck your emails before you hit "send".

Email Login Failure

You'll be required to change your password regularly. You'll need to contact your unit's communications representative to get your email reset. Do not wait until you need assistance to find out who you contact, find out who your contact is and write it below.

Email issues, contact:

(List Below)
_____

Fundamentals of Land Navigation

One of the most valuable skills to know, although you will likely use rarely, is the ability to navigate. Understanding this basic skill helps you understand map reading, as well as basic navigation

over, not only land, but water and even flight.

Roads, signs, and GPS laden navigation ensure that map and compass navigation are a lost art form, however, when an individual is lost in open Texas expanses, or even ranches, there might not be any roads. Remember that in a post-storm environment, signs, roads, and landmarks may not be present or obvious.

In order to measure something, there must always be a starting point or zero measurement. To express direction as a unit of angular measure, there must be a starting point or zero measure and a point of reference These

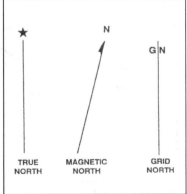

two points designate the base or reference line. There are three base lines— true north, magnetic north, and grid north. The most commonly used are magnetic and grid.

- ❖ **True North.** A line from any point on the earth's surface to the north pole. All lines of longitude are true north lines. True north is usually represented by a star.
- ❖ **Magnetic North.** The direction to the north magnetic pole, as indicated by the north-seeking needle of a magnetic instrument. The magnetic north is usually symbolized by a line ending with half of an arrowhead. Magnetic readings are obtained with magnetic instruments, such as lensatic and M2 compasses.
- ❖ **Grid North.** The north that is established by using the vertical grid lines on the map. Grid north may be symbolized by the letters GN or the letter "y".

The Compass

The **lensatic compass** is the most common and simplest instrument for measuring direction. The lensatic compass consists of three major parts: the cover, the base, and the lens.

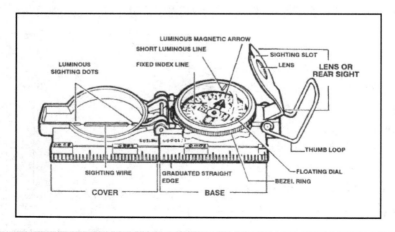

Base. The body of the compass contains the following movable parts:

(1) The floating dial is mounted on a pivot so it can rotate freely when the compass is held level. Printed on the dial in luminous figures are an arrow and the letters E and W. The arrow always points to magnetic north and the letters fall at east (E) 90° and west (W) 270° on the dial. There are two scales; the outer scale denotes mils and the inner scale (normally in red) denotes degrees.

(2) Encasing the floating dial is a glass containing a fixed black index line.

(3) The bezel ring is a ratchet device that clicks when turned. It contains 120 clicks when rotated fully; each click is equal to 3°. A short luminous line that is used in conjunction with the north-seeking arrow during navigation is contained in the glass face of the bezel ring.

(4) The thumb loop is attached to the base of the compass.

Lens. The lens is used to read the dial, and it contains the rear-sight slot used in conjunction with the front for sighting on objects. The rear sight also serves as a lock and clamps the dial when closed for its protection. The rear sight must be opened more than 45° to allow the dial to float freely.

Compass Handling

Compasses are delicate instruments and should be cared for accordingly.

a. **Inspection.** A detailed inspection is required when first obtaining and using a compass. One of the most important parts to check is the floating dial, which contains the magnetic needle. The user must also make sure the sighting wire is straight, the glass and crystal parts are not broken, the numbers on the dial are readable, and most important, that the dial does not stick.

b. **Effects of Metal and Electricity.** Metal objects and electrical sources can affect the performance of a compass. However, nonmagnetic metals and alloys do not affect compass readings. The following separation distances are suggested to ensure proper functioning of a compass:

High-tension power lines	55 meters.
Truck, Car,	18 meters.
Telephone wires and barbed wire	10 meters.
Metal water tank, or	2 meters.
Steel helmet or rifle	1/2 meter.

Accuracy. A compass is a precision instrument. They must be kept in good working condition is very accurate. However, a compass has to be checked periodically on a known line of direction, such as a surveyed azimuth using a declination station. Compasses with more than 3° + variation should not be used.

Protection. If traveling with the compass unfolded, make sure the rear sight is fully folded down onto the bezel ring. This will lock the floating dial and prevent vibration, as well as protect the crystal and rear sight from damage.

Azimuth

An azimuth is defined as a horizontal angle measured clockwise from a north base line. This north base line could be true north, magnetic north, or grid north. The azimuth is the most common military method to express direction. When using an azimuth, the point from which the azimuth originates is the center of an imaginary circle. This circle is divided into 360 degrees. Each degree represents an azimuth.

The military protractor represents the azimuth circle. The degree scale is graduated from 0 to 360 degrees; each tick mark on the degree scale represents one degree. A line from 0 to 180 degrees is called the base line of the protractor. Where the base line intersects the horizontal line, between 90 and 270 degrees, is the index or center of the protractor.

Distance

Not only is it vital to know the direction you are traveling, but also the Distance you are traveling. The US Military, most commonly utilizes meters (FOR LAND NAV). The most basic distance the individual must establish is '100 meters. Knowing 100 meters allows the navigator to approximate whether they have traveled 'less than 100 meters to a "klick." A klick is military speak for a kilometer (or 1000 meters).

To establish how far 100 meters is, set up two markers measured 100 meters apart and walk the distance, counting how many steps it takes to get

General Pace Count

- ❖ **100 Steps - On Flat Ground**
- ❖ **120 Steps – Walking Uphill**
- ❖ **110 Steps – Walking Downhill**

you from one to the other. Do this three times, average it out and you have established your **"Pace Count"**

Intersection

Intersection is the location of an unknown point by successively occupying at least two (preferably three) known positions on the ground and then map sighting on the unknown location. It is used to locate distant or inaccessible points or objects such as enemy targets and danger areas. There are two methods of intersection: the map and compass method and the straightedge method.

> *How it might work during emergency* [EXAMPLE]
>
> There is a lost person in an area. You see smoke from a camp fire that is approximately 4 or 5 miles away, you have a river and other terrain that will not allow you to get to them before darkness. A Helicopter will only be able to search for 10 minutes in the Dark before it must depart the area. You need to give the helicopter crew a pretty tight area to search.
>
> **WHAT YOU'LL DO:** First, you figure out your location on a map and use your compass to determine the azimuth where the smoke is emanating from. You'll then move to another location a mile or so away, and do the same thing. You will have two azimuths' that eventually intersect on your map. Where those lines intersect is where the smoke should be coming from; and where the helicopter should start searching.

How To; with a map and compass **(BASIC PROCESS)**

   a) Orient the map using the compass.
   b) Locate and mark your position on the map,

c) Determine the magnetic azimuth to the unknown position using the compass.
d) Draw a line on the map from your position on this azimuth.
e) Move to a second known point and repeat steps 1, 2, 3, 4, and 5.
f) The location of the unknown position is where the lines cross on the map.

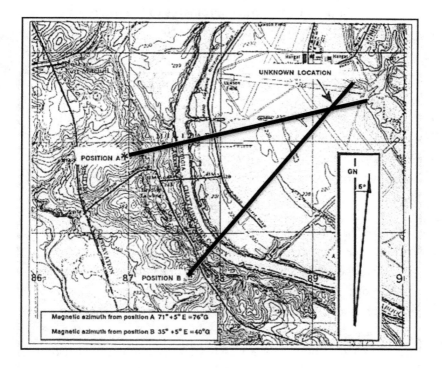

Resection

Resection is the method of locating one's position on a map by determining the grid azimuth to at least two well-defined locations that can be pinpointed on the map. For greater accuracy, the desired method of resection would be to use three or more well-defined locations.

How To; when using the map and compass **(BASIC PROCESS)**

   a) Orient the map using the compass.
   b) Identify two or three known distant locations on the ground and mark them on the map.
   c) Repeat 3, 4, and 5 for a second position and a third position, if desired.
   d) (7) The intersection of the lines is your location. Determine the grid coordinates to the desired accuracy.

How it might work during emergency **[EXAMPLE]**

You are lost (or do not know where you're at) and it's getting late in the day and there's a storm coming in. If you can't get to a campsite, you will have a really bad night in the woods… and there are lots of Mountain Lions reported in the area.

WHAT YOU WILL DO: First, you'll orient your map. Then you'll orient your compass to your map. You'll then find a landmark in the distance such as 's a tall mountain peak and locate it on your map. Whatever azimuth it is on, draw a line on your map through the general area you are located at. Find a second landmark such as a second mountain that is distinguishable on your map and shoot an azimuth in that direction as well. Draw it on your map and where the two lines intersect, is where you will be.

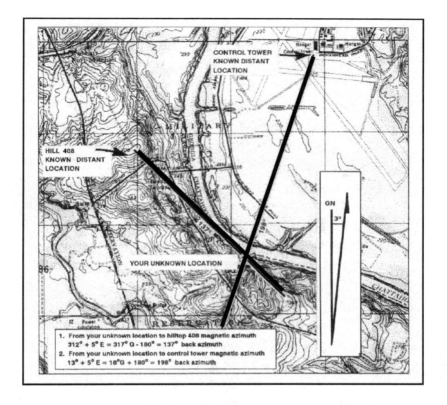

Global Positioning System (GPS)

The GPS is a satellite-based, global, all-weather, continuously available, radio positioning navigation system. It is highly accurate in determining position location derived from signal triangulation from a satellite constellation system. It is capable of determining latitude, longitude, and altitude of the individual user.

It is being fielded in hand-held, vehicular, aircraft, and watercraft configurations. The GPS receives and processes data from satellites on either a simultaneous or sequential basis. It measures the velocity and range with respect to each satellite, processes the data in terms of an earth-centered, earth-fixed coordinate system, and displays the information to the user in geographic or military grid coordinates.

   a. The GPS can provide precise steering information, as well as position location. The receiver can accept many checkpoints entered in any coordinate system by the user and convert them to the desired coordinate system. The user then calls up the desired checkpoint and the receiver will display direction and distance to the checkpoint. The GPS does not have inherent drift, an improvement over the Inertial Navigation System, and the receiver will automatically update its position. The receiver can also compute time to the next checkpoint.

   b. Specific uses for the GPS are position location; navigation; weapon location; target and sensor location; scout and screening operations; combat resupply; location of obstacles, barriers, and gaps; and communication support. The GPS also has the potential to allow units to train their soldiers and provide the following:

   The GPS is a satellite-based, radio navigational system. It consists of a constellation with 24 active satellites that interfaces with a ground-, air-, or sea-based receiver. Each satellite transmits data that enables the GPS receiver to provide precise position and time to the user. The GPS receivers come in several configurations, hand-held, vehicular-mounted, aircraft-mounted, and watercraft-mounted.
   GPS can locate the position of the user accurately to within 21 meters—95 percent of the time. However, the GPS has been known to accurately locate the position of the user within 8 to 10 meters. It can determine the distance and direction from the user to a programmed location or the distance between two

programmed locations called way points. It provides exact date and time for the time zone in which the user is located. The data supplied by the GPS is helpful in performing several techniques, procedures, and missions that require soldiers to know their exact location. Some examples are:

- Sighting.
- Surveying.
- Forward observing.
- Route planning and execution.
- Amphibious operations.

GPS Limitations

Like any system, GPS has some limitations. The satellites broadcast precise signals for use by navigational sets. The satellites are arranged in six rings that orbit the earth twice each day. The GPS navigational signals are similar to light rays, so anything that blocks the light will reduce or block the effectiveness of the signals. The more unobstructed the view of the sky, the better the system performs.

Operating On the Texas/Mexico Border

The Texas Border is a difficult area to work on and poses many natural, and human, threats to TXSG Members. The harsh conditions include:
- Extreme Heat
- Dirt and Sand
- Caliche
- The Rio Grande River
- Illegal Aliens
- Narcotics/Human Smugglers

Additional safety concerns include Illegal Alien activity as well as drug smugglers. Illegal Aliens do not generally seek to have

confrontations with personnel, and currently, they are not generally armed, however, Human and Narcotics Smuggling organizations have armed themselves to protect their profits and keep those being smuggled in control until they can be paid.

Much of the border has no fencing, however, there has been a push by the US Government to complete a fence where feasible. Currently, much of the border is based upon the Rio Grande river. Fencing varies from Concrete block, to

standard 7ft. chain-link fencing, to 12ft. Iron vertical. Unfortunately, in some areas, there may only be three strand barb wire cattle fencing, and in other areas, there will be no fencing. Some areas of the border have two types of fencing connecting to the other.

If the terrain or vegetation do not get, you can be certain that living threats will. Whether from large cats, insects, large birds, or packs of "Texas sized" Coyotes, feral hogs, or wild dogs, the border areas lead to death for many

of those who enter it. Regardless of whether it is smugglers and Illegal Aliens, or hikers, always be on guard.

Be careful and pay attention to your location when working near the border to ensure you do not illegally enter Mexico. It is likely that you will go to (Mexican) jail **IF** captured, seized, or detained.

Federal Emergency Management Agency

In order to standardize as much of the individual training as possible, and avoid re-creating the wheel, the decision was made to utilize external training sources that meet the needs of the TXSG. Basic courses in Emergency Management are not only the cornerstone of the TXSG, they are relevant to what is needed in actual emergencies. Federal Emergency Management Agency, or FEMA, training is the cornerstone of TXSG training.

FEMA's mission is to support our citizens and first responders to ensure that as a nation we work together to build, sustain and improve our capability to prepare for, protect against, respond to, recover from and mitigate all hazards.

FEMA's Independent Study Program offers courses that support the nine mission areas identified by the National Preparedness Goal. Those goals are:

1. Incident Management
2. Operation Planning
3. Disaster Logistics
4. Emergency Communications
5. Service to Disaster Victims
6. Continuity Programs
7. Public Disaster Communications
8. Integrated Preparedness
9. Hazard Mitigation

During times of emergency, the Texas State Guard provides support to those FEMA Missions, specifically its:

- Incident Management
- Emergency Communications
- Service to Disaster Victims

In addition, we work closely with local emergency management personnel from any number of Local, State, and Federal agencies. The language that is required when assisting in most emergencies, is that taught through FEMA. The FEMA Courses that all TXSG members are required to complete are:

FEMA 100	Introduction to Incident Command System (ICS)
FEMA 200	ICS for Single Resources and Initial Action Incident
FEMA 700	National Incident Management System (NIMS)
FEMA 800	National Response Framework, Introduction
FEMA 546	Continuity of Operations Awareness Course
FEMA 547	Introduction to Continuity of Operations
FEMA 775	EOC Management and Operations

These courses are online and can be found at:

www.training.fema.gov

⟶ Click the link for "**Independent Study.**"

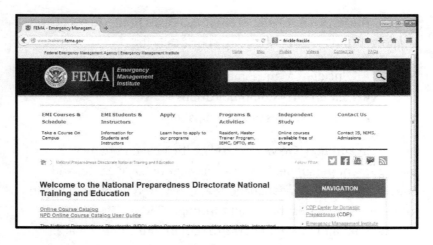

▬▶ Click the link for "**IS Course List**" on the left side of the page.

▬▶ Find and pick the course you want to take. You will need to register to get your certificate.

What to Do Next

Print and Save your Certificates as PDF documents and send them to the proper Points Of Contact within your unit. This is usually your unit training NCO or Officer.

NOTES:

_____

_____

_____

_____

List The Courses You've Taken and the Dates:

FEMA 100 _____

FEMA 200 _____

FEMA 300 _____

FEMA 400 _____

FEMA 700 _____

FEMA 800 _____

FEMA 546 _____

FEMA 547 _____

FEMA 775 _____

_____

_____

_____

_____

_____

_____

Common Spanish Words and Phrases

Texas shares a border with the country of Mexico and serves as the southern border of the United States. As such, the Spanish language is the language spoken within Mexico, and by a large number of people who've entered the United States (whether legally or illegally). It serves Texas State Guard personnel to familiarize themselves, or have access to some common Spanish phrases. Some Of those phrases might include:

ENGLISH	SPANISH	PRONOUNCIATION
Good morning	Buenos días	booEHN-os DEE-as
Good afternoon	Buenas tardes	booEHN-as TAR-dehs
Good evening (greeting)	Buenas noches	booEHN-as NO-chehs
Hello, my name is "John"	Hola, me llamo "Juan"	OH-la meh YA-mo "Wahn" [Replace John/Juan/Wahn with your name]
What is your name	Cómo se llama usted	KOH-moh seh YA-mah oos-TEHD
How are you	Cómo está usted	KOH-moh ehs-TA oos-TEHD
I am fine	Estoy bien	ehs-TOY bee-EHN
Goodbye	Adiós	ah-dee-OHS
Please	Por favor	pohr fah-VOR
Halt / Stop	Alto	Ahl Toh
I do not understand	Yo no comprendo	yoh no kom-PREN-doh
Thank you	Gracías	gra-SEE-ahs
I'm sorry	Lo siento	low see-EHN-to

You are welcome (it was nothing)	De nada	deh NA-da
How many are there	Cuántos hay	kooAN-tohs eye
Yes	Sí	see
No	No	no
Bad	Malo	Mah Loh
What time is it	Qué hora es	keh OR-ah ehs
Police	Policia	Pol Lee See Ah
One moment	Uno momento	Uhn No Mo ment Oh
Who	Quièn	kee-EHN
Why	Por què	pohr keh

NOTES:

Firearms Identification & Safety

Although The TXSG is not currently an armed service because the State of Texas does not currently require another armed force. The future needs of Texas may require such capability. Many of our members train with, qualify on, and even compete in firearms competitions such as the Governor's 20*. The Governors Twenty are the twenty best marksmen in the Texas Military Forces. Personnel compete on behalf of the Texas Commander-In-Chief.

However, as military personnel, it is incumbent upon us to understand firearms, and the use of firearms in a manner that represents us. Besides, we are Texans and it is our nature to understand the employment of the firearm. Additionally, Future TXSG leadership may choose to utilize firearms in a different way. TXSG is always one incident away from firearms.

As an example, In the 1940's TXSG was issued Rifles, Machine Guns, and Armored Vehicles from the War Department to help defend the country as US military forces deployed to fight overseas. The TXSG, and other State Defense Forces, protected the homeland with firearms.

General Firearm Type Identification

Firearms are generally similar in operation, and in spite of looking vastly different, there are certain features that identify certain classes of firearms. The type of firearm is based upon its action, or how it loads and cycles ammunition. Additional factors include what type of ammunition the firearm fires.

Firearms are extremely customizable. Although general descriptions are used below, it should be recognized that most features can be utilized on other firearm types. As a basic example; Semi-Automatic Rifles may have hunting scopes on them, or a shotgun may have a pistol grip similar to that of a Semi-Automatic sporting Rifle.

Semi-Auto Rifle

The Semi-automatic rifle is sometimes erroneously dubbed an "Assault Rifle". Although most firearms that society labels Assault Rifles do not operate like the military definition of an Assault Rifles. They do, however, have contemporary, technilogical features that actual Assault Rifles may have such as: flash hiders, adjustable stocks, pistol grips, and detachable magazines. Features that may distinguish many Semi-Auto rifles would be:

- Generally Black in color
- Detachable Magazines
- Pistol Grips
- Semi-Automatic operations
- Magazine/Shot capacity of 10-30 rounds

Semi-auto rifles use gases captured from fired bullets to operate the action and prepare the rifle to fire the next round.

Bolt-Action Rifle

Hunting rifles are usually identifiable by their shapes. They use a traditional stock shapes. Hunting rifles tend to have Bolt Actions. This requires the shooter to manually cycle the action before firing each shot. Features that distinguish many Bolt Action rifles would include:

- Stock made of wood are common
- Tactical/police versions may be black or camouflage
- Scope for long-range targeting and shooting
- Long and slender shape
- A handle on the side of the rifle above the trigger

Hunting rifles are the high-powered basis of the modern military Sniper Rifle. They may be black or camouflaged.

Revolver

Revolvers are handguns in which a cylinder in the center rotates and aligns bullets to the barrel. In effect, revolvers have a chamber for each round it can hold in its cylinder.

- Rotating Cylinder
- 5-7 rounds between reloads
- Generally Silver, Nickel, Chrome, or black in color

Pump Action Shotgun

Pump action shotguns are still the most common type of shotgun, despite the many new semi-auto shotguns on the market currently. Pump shotguns vary widely, depending upon their usage. Some of the distinguishing features may be:
- 38-51 Inches in length
- A tube magazine under the barrel
- 6-9 shots before reload is required
- That unmistakable pump sound between shots
- Tactical Shotguns tend to be black.
- Wood stocks are still common.
- That distinctive pump sound that ALL Americans recognize as danger.

Auto-Pistol

Auto pistols are handguns that replaced the revolver as the standard type of handgun action throughout the world. Some of the standard features of auto pistols might include:
- Detachable Magazine
- 9-16 Rounds before reloading
- 4.5-6.5 inches long

Firearms Safety (The Five Rules)

Although we are Texans, and most of us have experience with firearms, it never hurts to point out some obvious Firearms Safety rules.

The Five GOLDEN Rules Of Firearms Safety

1. Treat ALL firearms as though they are loaded until cleared (ensured empty)
2. Never handle a firearm that you do not know how to safely operate.
3. NEVER point a firearm at something you do not intend to shoot, destroy, and/or kill.
4. Clear the firearm before transporting.
5. Keep your finger off the trigger until ready to fire.

Governor's Twenty

The Governor's Twenty Tab is a state-level marksmanship award worn on the uniforms of very few of us. Marksmanship competition determines the best 20 marksmen within the Texas Military Forces.

Guardsmen compete in Pistol (8 shooters), Rifle (8 shooters), Sniper (a team of 2), and Machine Gun (2 gunners).

The Texas State Guard has done well in competition since it has competed. TXSG teams have amazingly secured the top position in Pistol, Rifle, and Sniper, over Army National Guard, and Air National Guard shooters.

Self-Aid and Buddy Care

First Aid Kit

It is important to have access to a First Aid kit. Being prepared may save the life of yourself or other TXSG members, or ensure minor injuries do not become infected or progress into more significant injuries. It is not necessary to purchase entire kits. It is simple enough to purchase the items to make a simple First Aid Kit. First Aid kits may include:

- Assorted Band-Aids
- Sterile gauze pads
- 3 pair of medical gloves (non-latex)
- First-aid tape
- Aspirin and ibuprofen
- Hydrocortisone
- 2 compress dressings (5 x 9 inches)
- 2 elastic bandages
- Antibiotic ointment
- 2 triangular bandages (for making slings)
- Cold pack
- Oral thermometer, scissors, tweezers

SELF AID and BUDDY CARE are continually updated with new techniques and procedures. As such, it is important that you get trained by your unit and prepare for any case in which you may need to know Self Aid:

THE BELOW INFORMATION IS A BASIC GUIDE ONLY.

Basic Life Saving Steps:

1

Establish an open airway/Ensure breathing. Lack of oxygen intake through breathing can lead to death in a very few minutes.

2

Stop bleeding to support circulation.

3

Prevent further disability. By dressing and bandaging wounds, you are avoiding infection, suffering, and further damage. For example, by splinting a broken limb, you are keeping sharp bone ends from causing unnecessary nerve and tissue damage. Immobilize neck injuries.

4

Minimize further Exposure to adverse weather.

5

Treat for Shock

Bleeding (External/Internal)

When the skin is damaged or punctured, the circulatory system continues to function and forces blood from the inside of the body through any available holes. This is the process we call bleeding. There is also a type of bleeding that occurs when internal organs are damaged, but the skin is not punctured so the blood remains internally. As such, the two types of bleeding are external and internal.

External Bleeding

The 3 types of External Bleeding are:

- ➤ Arterial bleeding. Bright Red, high oxygen content. Spurting with each contraction or pulse of the heart.
- ➤ Venous bleeding. Dark red - low oxygen content and steady flow
- ➤ Capillary bleeding. Continuous steady ooze.

There are four ways to control External Bleeding:

1) Direct Pressure
2) Elevation
3) Pressure Points
4) Tourniquet

Direct Pressure is when you apply steady, even pressure to an injury. To do this, use a sterile/clean material (as available) with your hand. Once you start, do not remove dressings until medical help arrives. If the dressing becomes soaked, add more dressings and pressure. Do not remove old blood-soaked dressings.

Elevate the bleeding injury as high as feasible to allow gravity to help in minimizing the blood flowing to the area. Elevation is used in conjunction with direct pressure.

Pressure Points are points that blood must flow past in order to travel down the limbs. There are 2 main pressure points that we use:

    (1) Arm - (brachial) inner half of arm midway between the elbow and armpit.

    (2) Leg - (femoral) compress the femoral artery with the heel of your hand.

Tourniquets are used for severe bleeding. They are only used as a **LAST RESORT** because they will lead to damage of the tissue, nerves, and blood vessels. Use a tourniquet that is at least 2 inches wide. Place the tourniquet around the limb, between the wound and heart. Never place a tourniquet below the elbow or knee. Tighten enough to stop bleeding. Once a tourniquet is in place, leave it there. Do not disturb it, mark a "T", and the time (if feasible) on the victims head to alert medical personnel when it was placed. Transport the victim with the tourniquet exposed to medical personnel, as quickly as possible. Time will determine if the limb survives or will be amputated.

Internal Bleeding

    There are some situations in which the body falls, is crushed, or is impacted with blunt objects that do not penetrate the skin. In these cases, it is possible that the trauma will lead to internal bleeding, in which the internal organs are damaged, but the blood does not escape the body. This can cause internal bleeding.

Internal Bleeding is usually not visible, but there may be some signs of it. Some of the more common signs and symptoms are:

- Bleeding from any opening in the body, (i.e. ear, nose, and mouth).
- Bruising,
- Skin may become cold, clammy or pale.
- Pupils may be dilated
- Nausea or vomiting.

If an individual is bleeding internally, they will still bleed to death. As blood escapes the circulatory system, blood pressure will drop and the individual will die just as though the blood is escaping the body. Get anyone suspected of internal bleeding to medical professionals immediately. To control Internal Bleeding:

- Bleeding within the chest. If breathing is not impaired, apply a wide, bandage around the chest. Treat for shock.
- Abdominal bleeding. Abdomen will be rigid and warm. Apply wide bandage and fit snugly, but do not interfere with breathing. Treat for shock.
- Bleeding into extremities. Area will be warm and swollen, treat by splinting. Treat for shock.

Blood-Borne Phathogens

Blood-borne Pathogens are disease producing agents or microorganisms that can become present in human blood or other potentially infectious materials. These agents can be transmitted between humans. Some well documented blood-borne

pathogens include; Human Immunodeficiency Virus (HIV), Hepatitis B, and Tuberculosis.

To avoid exposure to such pathogens, you must:

- ✓ Treat all blood and bodily fluids as potentially infectious whenever they are encountered.
- ✓ Modify your behavior at accident scenes to avoid exposure to bodily fluids.
- ✓ Always wear surgical gloves (Personal Protective Equipment, PPE) when blood is present.
- ✓ Always decontaminate your hands and equipment using an appropriate cleanser (or diluted bleach) when exposed.
- ✓ Report all injuries involving puncture wounds and contact with body fluids such as needle sticks, human bites, and lacerations.

If on TXSG Orders, you are required to inform your supervision, mission leader, chain of command, and/or contact the TXSG Medical Brigade for information and follow medical recommendations regarding care.

Heat Injuries

Texas gets "Texas Hot". Temperatures can reach 110-115 degrees Fahrenheit in some areas of Texas during the summer months. The highest (recorded) temperature was 120.6 in the year of 1936, in Seymour, Baylor County.

Heat injuries kill by pushing the human body beyond its ability to dissipate heat and maintain a reasonable body temperature. In extreme heat and high humidity, evaporation causes "sweating" to become ineffective, and the body must work extra hard to maintain a life-sustaining temperature, and the body begins to fail and die.

When the body runs dry of fluids, Dehydration is the result. Symptoms of dehydration include:

- Dry Mouth
- Headache
- Dizziness

The go-to action once a person realizes they are dehydrated is to intake WATER, and cool down for a few minutes or even hours, if necessary.

Heat Exhaustion and Heat Stroke

The two main Heat Injuries TXSG members may come in contact with include, Heat Exhaustion, and Heat Stroke. Most heat injuries occur when an individual is overexposed and over-worked beyond his/her physical condition. "Older", overweight, environmentally exposed, less physically fit, or dehydrated individuals are at the greatest risk.

Heat Exhaustion is a medical condition. It CAN be remedied without an ambulance. Some of the symptoms include:

- ✓ Dizziness
- ✓ Headache
- ✓ Nausea
- ✓ Weakness
- ✓ Clumsy/Unsteady Movement
- ✓ Muscle Cramps

Treat Heat Exhaustion by, (1) Resting out of the sun, (2) Loosening the victims clothing, (3) Rehydrating with water or popular sports drinks (such as Gatorade). Ensure that we observe and evacuate the victim if their condition does not quickly improve.

Heat Stroke IS ALWAYS A MEDICAL EMERGENCY. Because brain function has become compromised, the condition may become fatal. Symptoms include:

- ✓ Profuse Sweating
- ✓ Convulsions and Chills
- ✓ Vomiting
- ✓ Confusion and Mumbling
- ✓ Combative
- ✓ Passing Out

The only action to be taken is to **Cool and Call**. The damage is already done. The victim MUST BE COOLED DOWN IMMEDIATELY. This is done by, (1) Removing Clothing, (2) Cold Water or Ice, (3) Fanning, and (4) Calling for evacuation. You CAN NOT waste time to determine if the individual is going to stabilize.

Shock

"Shock" is the collapse of the cardiovascular system. The Cardiovascular system is the network of the body that provides circulation of blood, and oxygen to the body. Shock is a biologic process that forces the body to slow down and limit blood flow to any injuries the body may have. Signs and Symptoms of shock could include:

- Restlessness and anxiety.
- Pulse - weak and rapid.
- Skin - cold, clammy, and pale.

- Sweating - profuse.
- Respirations - shallow, labored and rapid.
- Eyes - dull with pupils dilated and slow to react.
- Thirst (Do not give fluids to drink only wet the lips with water).
- Nausea and vomiting.

Dressings and Bandages

A dressing is a sterile pad used to cover a wound. Bandages are used to hold dressings in place. To apply a dressing as a bandage, cut/tear clothing away from the wound, place the dressing over wound, secure dressing over wound, apply the bandage tight enough to keep dressing from slipping, but not so tight as to interfere with circulation. Improvised bandages can be made out of items such as:

- ❖ Belts.
- ❖ Rifle Sling.
- ❖ Handkerchiefs.
- ❖ Strips of clothing.

Fractures

There are two types, Open and Closed. An Open Fracture is where the bone penetrates the skin (can be seen). A Closed Fracture does not penetrate the skin. If you are not able to determine a fracture from the victim, some signs of a fracture would include:

- Deformity.
- Tenderness.
- Grating.
- Swelling and discoloration.

Splinting

In the case of a fracture or broken bone; when medical personnel are not readily available, it may be necessary to secure a broken bone. Splinting prevents motion on fragments or fractured bones. It may reduce pain and prevents further damage of muscles, nerves and vessels.

Remove clothing from area of fracture, splint above and below the joint, or break, involved, "Splint them where they lie." Use padding between the injured bone and the splint. Secure the splint with bandages at several points above and below the fracture, use a sling to support splinted arm. Some improvised splints might include:

- Boards
- Poles
- Sticks
- Cardboard
- Tree limbs
- Rolled Newspapers/Magazines

Burns

Burns cause tissue damage by excessive exposure to thermal heat, electricity, chemicals and radiant heat. There are 3 degrees of burns:

1) First Degree: Redness, Swelling, Moderate Pain.

2) Second Degree: Has blisters and wet appearance.

-- Most painful because of irritated nerve endings in dermis

3) Third Degree: Destruction of tissue.

-- Little pain (except bordering areas).

-- Charred or waxy white appearance.

General treatment for burns:

Regarding burns, there is not much the general first responder can take. What we can do is minimize the damage and get the individual to a proper medical facility. Attempt to:

- Remove victim from the heat source by cooling the burn if still hot, but do not chill the patient.
- Clear the wound unless clothing sticks by removing constricting clothing and jewelry. DO NOT put butter, creams or salves on the wound.
- Cover with a sterile dressing.

Compression Only CPR

Hands-Only CPR is using chest compressions without the mouth-to-mouth resuscitation that was previously used in "CPR". performed by a bystander has been shown to be as effective as conventional CPR (CPR that includes breaths) in the first few minutes of an out-of-hospital sudden cardiac arrest.

Compression only CPR is important because history and actual cases show that many people will not give mouth-to-mouth resuscitation to strangers. Additionally, we've learned that mouth-to-mouth is not as effective as previously believed. It is important because ANY attempt at CPR is better than no attempt. The purpose of all CPR is to use the heart as a manual pump to start, and maintain, the blood flowing through the body.

What Are the Components of Take 10?

> **Take 10 – Compression ONLY CPR**
>
> 1. **CHECK**: For signs of life (responsiveness, normal breathing)
>
> 2. **CALL**: Call 911
>
> 3. **COMPRESS**: Hard and fast, center of chest...

(Step 1) Check

If an individual has a heart attack, he/she will drop and you must ***check*** to see if you can find a heartbeat. If you cannot, you will **check** to see if they are breathing. If they are not, you must make the decision to begin Take10 Compression only CPR.

Immediately after establishing that you have a medical emergency, be cognizant of the fact that many public places have Automated Defibrillators. Automated Defibrillators are generally located in boxes hanging on walls, perhaps near fire alarms. The directions generally require placing two leads onto a victim's chest and sending a electrical current into a body!

(Step 2) Call

After determining that there is an emergency, you or anyone nearby, must call for help (Dial 911) immediately to get Emergency responders on the way as soon as possible. It may take them awhile to get to you. Every moment counts. If there is no heartbeat, the decision must be made to initiate chest compressions.

(Step 3) Compress

Place your hands in the center of the chest, one hand behind the other and begin to compress the chest roughly 1.5-2 inches at about 100 beats per minute. Use the popular disco song by the Bee Gees, "Staying Alive" (1977) as a reference. Be cognizant that you WILL LIKELY hear a cracking noise but continue compressing. The cracking sound is normal!

DO NOT STOP until emergency personnel arrive. Compressions will utilize the heart as a pump, and blood will slowly begin pumping around the body (and brain). If you stop, the pumping action will stop and the blood will stop moving around the body. Once you start pumping again, the blood will slowly start moving again. It is imperative that the blood does NOT stop circulating once it has started.

Most people will become exhausted after only a few minutes, but compressions must continue. If someone else is near, ask that they take over compressions. Continue compressions until paramedics arrive. Do NOT stop! When you get tired find someone else to continue.

Heart Attack vs. Sudden Cardiac Arrest

Heart Attacks and Sudden Cardiac Arrest are NOT the same. Heart Attacks are a problem with pumping ability, while the Sudden Cardiac Arrest are a problem with the heart muscle quivering. Either way, death may be minutes away.

Heart Attack

Heart Attacks are caused by blockages. The heart is a muscle and needs oxygen to thrive. When blood flow that brings oxygen to the heart is cut or reduced by fat or cholesterol (plaque) a heart attack occurs as the heart muscles dies. As the heart dies, blood to the rest of the body dies.

Sudden Cardiac Arrest

Cardiac Arrest (or Sudden Cardiac Death/SCD) is when the heart's electrical system malfunctions and the heart stops pumping regularly due to abnormal, or irregular, heart rhythm (arrhythmias). CPR (cardiopulmonary resuscitation) may be performed until a defibrillator is located and used. In the moment, it may not be clear what, medically, is occurring. Action will need to be taken.

Defibrillation is where an electronic device sends a shock to the heart. This electric shock helps the heart to get on a normal contraction rhythm. Defibrillators are compact and may already hang on many commercial building walls near fire extinguishers or fire alarms. Alternatively, they may be labeled as Automated External Defibrillators (AEDs).

The Automated External Defibrillators (AEDs) vary by manufacturer, however, are simple to use. Modern AEDs have a 3-Step process that will include instruction on where to place the pads on the victim's chest. The AED will monitor seek a heartbeat, it will build a voltage charge, and finally, it will tell you to push the (generally green) button on the unit, and will give you a countdown, and friendly reminder to keep your hands clear of the victim.

Fatigue

During emergency operations, TXSG members may be tasked to work for extended periods of time without relief. Fatigue can become a risk factor of safe operations. Most humans, require 7 to 8 hours of actual, quality sleep every 24 hours to function efficient and effectively.

Working on behalf of those who need assistance, such as in a disaster area leads most people to strive to put in extensive hours. But it is important to understand that with poor sleep, comes a degradation in performance, both mentally and physically. Eventually, people may seem confused and may not think effectively, or as quickly as their situation may dictate. Lack of sleep may increase the risk of falls, or car automotive collisions.

Used as a form of torture, sleep deprivation will increase the risk of deadly mistakes, and will even negatively affect long-term health. Signs of fatigue include:

- Difficulty focusing
- Frequent blinking,
- heavy eyelids, and eye-rubbing
- Repeated yawning
- Feeling restless and irritable

It is incumbent on all members to pay attention to co-workers and identify any signs of fatigue and take action. Failure to act may lead to fatigue based accidents and incidents. Do not let those showing signs of extreme fatigue to conduct critical activities such as operating cars, trucks… or buses. Relieve those who appear critically fatigued, and allow them to take a nap, and recharge before continuing.

As volunteers, some will continue to work longer than they should, and that is commendable, BUT, allowing severely fatigued individuals to do so, can become a risk to others, and the mission at hand if they are making non-positive decisions.

Height and Weight Table

Height and Weight is becoming ever more important within the TXSG. These measurements are now being used to determine if members are eligible for promotion. Regardless, it is our duty to strive to meet and maintain the height and weight standards.

MEN: Height and Weight Table					
		Maximum Weight			
Height (inches)	Minimum Weight	17-20 years	21-27 years	28-39 years	40 years and over
60	100	160	162	164	167
61	102	166	168	170	174
62	103	170	173	176	179
63	104	176	178	182	185
64	105	182	184	188	191
65	106	187	190	193	197
66	107	193	196	199	204
67	111	200	202	206	209
68	115	206	208	212	215
69	119	212	214	217	222
70	123	217	221	224	229
71	127	223	227	231	235
72	131	230	233	237	242
73	135	236	239	244	248
74	139	243	246	251	255
75	143	250	253	258	262
76	147	256	260	265	269
77	151	263	267	271	276
78	153	270	274	278	284
79	159	277	281	285	290
80	166	284	288	293	298

Height (inches)	Minimum Weight	Maximum Weight			
		17-20 years	21-27 years	28-39 years	40 years and over
58	90	129	132	137	140
59	92	133	137	141	145
60	94	138	141	146	146
61	96	143	146	151	155
62	98	148	152	158	160
63	100	153	158	162	166
64	102	158	162	167	170
65	104	162	167	171	176
66	106	168	173	177	182
67	109	171	177	183	186
68	112	177	183	189	192
69	115	182	187	193	198
70	118	187	193	199	204
71	122	192	198	204	209
72	125	198	204	210	216
73	128	204	209	216	222
74	130	210	217	223	228
75	133	216	223	230	235
76	136	223	230	237	240
77	139	229	236	243	247
78	141	235	242	248	253
79	144	240	247	255	260
80	147	246	253	261	267

WOMEN: Height and Weight Table

*** Both of these charts are subject to change at the discretion of the Texas State Guard.

Tax Implications

As the TXSG is a volunteer organization. Some of your costs associated with duty may be tax deductible. It is incumbent upon you to maintain records and accurately deduct your costs associated with you State duty. Utilize the chart below to collect your costs, and log and track your mileage, as it is tax-deductible.

YOU WILL BE ABLE TO DEDUCT YOUR COSTS... IF YOU SUBMIT YOUR ITEMIZED DEDUCTIONS. If you do not itemize your costs (which you should), you will not be able to deduct your costs of your efforts with the TX State Guard and your other pursuits.

What can you deduct?

- **Mileage**
- **Uniform Purchase, Maintenance, upkeep**
- **Equipment purchased for duty**
- **THIS BOOK (If Purchased)**

It is your responsibility to faithfully document your tax implications. Doing so will ensure you are not attempting to remember this information when it comes time to complete your taxes. <u>Always keep your receipts</u> or documentation. The information you will need to track for your taxes will be the:

1. Purchase Date
2. Item Being Purchased
3. The Item Cost

Be specific, maintain your tax records for 7 years, and as always, confirm with your tax software or tax preparer to ensure you are getting all of your LEGAL deductions.

Date/Month	Miles	Uniform	Other Costs

Common TXSG Jargon and Abbreviations

ACC	Army Component Command
ANCOC	Advanced Non-Commissioned Officer Course
BN	Battalion
BNCOC	Basic Non-Commissioned Officer Course
BOT	Basic Orientation Training
BSOC	Border Security Operations Center
CMSgt	Chief Master Sergeant
CCMSgt	Command Chief Master Sergeant
CDR	Commander
CG	Commanding General
CH	Chaplain
Chow	Meal
CMO	Chief Medical Officer
CNO	Chief Nursing Officer
CO	Commanding Officer
COC / CoC	Chain Of Command
Component	Specific Section of the TXSG -- Army, Air, Medical, or Maritime
CSM	Command Sergeant Major
CUB	Commander's Uniform Briefing
DFAC	Dining FACility
DPS	Department Of Public Safety
EOC	Emergency Operations Center
FEMA	Federal Emergency Management Administration
Head/Latrine	Bathroom,
IAP	Incident Action Plan
JAG	Judge Advocate General
METL	Mission Essential Task List
NCO	Non-Commissioned Officer

NCOIC	NCO In Charge
OCS	Officer Candidate School
OIC	Officer In Charge
PAB	Personnel Action Board
PLDC	Primary Leadership Development Course
PME	Professional Military Education
POC	Point Of Contact
PPE	Personal Protective Equipment
SEA	Senior Enlisted Advisor
SITREP	Situation Report
SOC	State Operations Center
SOC	State Operations Center
SOP	Standard Operating Procedures
TAG	Texas Adjutant General
TDEM	Texas Department of Emergency Management
Texas Military Forces	Combined Military Forces Of The State Of Texas
TICP	Texas Interoperability Communication protocol
TMAR	Texas Maritime Regiment
TOC	Tactical Operations Center
UMD	Unit Manning Document
XO	Executive Officer
REGT	Regiment

TXSG Benefits and Information

Texas Specific Holiday Schedule

In addition to Religious and/or Federal holidays, the State of Texas recognizes some additional unique holidays based upon our Texas History. These holidays include:

January 19	Confederate Heroes Day	Honors those Americans who fought for the Confederacy
March 2	Texas Independence Day	Recognizes those who fought for the Independence of Texas from Mexico
April 21	San Jacinto Day	The Decisive Battle of the Texas Revolution. 18 Minutes; 11 Texans Dead; 630 Mexicans Dead; 300 Mexicans Captured
June 19	Emancipation Day	Recognizes and honors the emancipation of the slaves in Texas in 1865
27 August	Lyndon Baines Johnson Day	Recognizes the Birthday of Lyndon Baines Johnson

State Tuition Reimbursement Program

The State Tuition Reimbursement Program is a state funded tuition assistance program for active drilling members of the Texas Army National Guard (TXARNG), Texas Air National Guard (TXANG), and Texas State Guard (TXSG). This education benefit provides up to $9,000 annually ($4,500-fall and $4,500-spring) in tuition and fees at an eligible Texas college or university. It may be used by:

- Active drilling members in "Good Standing" with TXARNG, TXANG or TXSG.
- Completed Basic Training. TXSG must complete BOT, RBOT or AIT.
- Enlisted (E1-E9), Officers (O1-O5), and Warrant Officers (WO1-CW3).
- Eligible school must be a public or private Texas State college or university with headquarters in Texas as defined in Texas Education Code Section 61.003. For profit schools are not eligible.
- Must have, and maintain, a 2.0 cumulative GPA.
- Must be accepted and registered in a qualifying college or university for a minimum of 3 semester credit hours.
- ROTC Cadets utilizing the Room & Board scholarship option.

Once applied for and accepted, the Tuition Programs serves as a tuition reimbursement. Once approved, you will pay for the courses and your money will be reimbursed. For more information, visit: **https://www.txmf.us/txmf-strp**.

TXSG Handgun License Program

Every member of the Texas State Guard is entitled to a free Texas Concealed Carry License. You will be required to submit your online application, submit your Fingerprints (FAST). You, of course, are still required to complete all other requirements, including your training, range, and fingerprinting.

When filing out the online form list "TXSG" when asked about your military affiliation and the fee will be reduced, pending your military Identification card.

Free TX Hunting License

If you are a hunter, you are entitled to a free yearly Texas State Hunting license. Go to a local hunting supply store and provide your ID Card. You are required to complete a Hunters Safety course prior to receiving your license.

Contact your unit for more information on this State benefit.

TX State Guard License Plate

If so interested, members of the TXSG may choose to get a Minuteman on their license plates.

Contact your unit, get the appropriate form. Request a signature from your commander. Once approved and signed by your chain of command, you will then need to take the form with you when you register your vehicle.

TX Military Department ID Card

Your State Guard ID card is not only a requirement for TXSG activities, it may also be used as a benefit in some cases. Many companies gladly give military discounts to those who serve the state of Texas. Some members save hundreds of dollars per year from companies such as Home Depot and Restaurants who give military discounts on meals.

NOTE: Military Discounts are a benefit from a company. If they choose not to honor those discounts; be courteous, say thank you and press on.

About This Handbook

The goals of this Handbook are to:

- Provide useful and relevant information
- Provide a training topics baseline/standard
- Provide Quick Reference
- Provide a measure of continuity
- Provide some historic context
- And to establish a framework to be built upon

DISCLAIMER

The Texas State Guard (TXSG) does not have an "official" handbook. This handbook should be treated as any commercially available guide or manual. All information within this document is Open Source, and publicly available. All information within this handbook is to be utilized as a quick reference guide. Confirm all information with TXSG policy, and unit procedures.

Any photos used are the property of the individuals who captured them. Photos were utilized directly because of their Public Domain status. Non-Public Domain photos, taken by TXSG members while under State of Texas orders, become public domain. Images posted to the Defense Video & Imagery Distribution System (DVIDS) are labeled under DVIDS as, "free of known copyright restrictions under U.S. copyright law"; and are expressly established as Public Domain.

CPSIA information can be obtained
at www.ICGtesting.com
Printed in the USA
LVHW081253241220
675062LV00030B/354